# Life in the modern world

**Mark J. Link, S.J.**

**home**
**parish**
**neighborhood**
**school**

**LOYOLA UNIVERSITY PRESS**
Chicago  60657

Library of Congress Catalog Card Number: 78-108376
ISBN 0-8294-0184-9
© 1969, 1970 Loyola University Press

## IN GRATITUDE

The author and Loyola University Press are deeply grateful to the following writers and their publishers for permission to quote from their works. All formal acknowledgments are listed on pages 263-65.

| | |
|---|---|
| Alexis Carrel | Jack Miles |
| Rian Clancy | Floyd Miller |
| Maurice Cooney | Elizabeth Mulligan |
| Roy Harrell, Jr. | Vernon Pizer |
| William Henry | Ralph Prouty |
| Joy Marie Hoag | Patrick Strickler |
| Nancy Konesko | John Travis |
| Robert Lambert | Phyllis Wiggins |
| Albert Lesco | Irene Wray |

# CONTENTS

SCHEMATIC OUTLINE

# CHAPTER 1

# FOUR WORLDS

Your personality is being shaped
within your four teen-age worlds.

## 1 YOUTH TODAY

Some people say that high-school students rarely think about the important things of life. They say that teen-agers are concerned only with sports, movies, and good times. The people who say this are clearly out of touch with young people.

It is true that young people are keenly interested in sports, movies, and having a good time. This is only natural. But many a young person will tell you that after he has finished studying or while walking home after a movie, he frequently finds himself thinking about life and what it means.

### Concerned

Many young people today are deeply concerned about life and what role they will some day play in it. It is a rare boy or girl who has not, occasionally, wondered whether he or she will be successful and happy ten or twenty years from now.

The question automatically arises: is there any way of foretelling whether you will be a successful adult?

One of the best guides to foretelling the future is to study the present. This is the idea behind the saying, "Well begun is half done." This means that if you are a successful teen-ager, you will probably be a successful adult. But this only raises a bigger question: how can you tell whether you are a successful teen-ager or not?

In response to this question, one educator said, "Show me how a young person responds to the challenges of his home, school, parish, and neighborhood; and, I will tell you how well he is growing into adulthood." This is another way of saying that every young person shapes his personality within his four teen-age worlds: home, school, parish, and neighborhood. To determine how well a young person is developing, we must take a look at him and his activity in these four worlds.

1 How would you rate these four worlds in the order of their importance in your own life? Explain why.

### Personality growth

This year's course will be divided into four sections. Each will deal with one of the four worlds in which you are living. Naturally these four worlds, or communities, overlap one another. But, in general, they provide an excellent framework for exploring teen-age life in the modern world.

Just as last year's course dealt with personality growth, so will this year's course. This year's program will be linked with last year's in still another way.

Last year, one of our goals was to discover what it means to be a Christian in the contemporary world. This year we will carry this one step further. We will see how a Christian reacts to the challenges he meets in the four worlds in which he lives.

2 How do the four worlds in which we live interact and influence one another? To what extent are we victims of our environment (worlds)? Can one world make up for defects in another? Explain.

## 2 AM I TYPICAL?

A Chicago sophomore describes
his four teen-age worlds.

I will start with my parish. I feel it is the least important
world I live in. To me it's just a place to go for one hour on
Sunday. The teen club is poorly run, and the people who go there
are not my type.

There are usually only two times (besides Sunday) that I go
anywhere near my parish. This is when our usual hangouts are
closed or when I play ball with some of the guys I hang around
with. These guys are not doopers or greasers but just plain sports-
minded guys. I'm usually with these guys during the day, but at
night I hang around with my greaser friends.

### Home world

Next would come my home. I come from an average middle-
class family. My grandmother lives in a special addition built
for her. When I was younger, my mother kept me sissified, and
my grandmother brought me up in the old-fashioned way. I was
a good student; and a good patrol boy, never late at my post; and
a good altar boy, never failed to show up, and I gladly substituted
for any guy because they told me it was an honor; never disobeyed
my elders; went to confession once a month. At the end of the
seventh grade, I was my parents' pride and joy and the most miserable guy in the neighborhood.

That summer I changed more drastically than I then believed. I adopted a why-give-a-damn attitude. I decided I would pick my own clothes, wear my hair the way I wanted to, hang around with the guys I wanted to; and, in short, do what I wanted to do.

In eighth grade I learned to copy, cheat, and cram. I tried to get away with everything from homework to altar boys. I no longer took everything sitting down; I began to fight back. Since then my homelife has completely changed. Now I am a sophomore in high school, and although my parents are still strict on some matters, I just say, "yes," and do what I want.

3 How typical would you say this boy's home situation is? Why is it that some teen-agers adjust to adolescence more smoothly than others?

### Neighborhood world

Next, and most important, comes my neighborhood. I think I described it pretty well in class. But there are a few things I would like to add. During the day I am a dooper. At night I'm a greaser, because the guys I hang around with then are greasers.

The distinction between dooper and greaser is not just clothes, but also the way you talk, act; in short, your whole personality. You could say the greasers have been around. They know what the world is like; and the doopers are the ones who stay in their sheltered little worlds. When you're a greaser, you don't act tough, because if you do you're phony. You are tough. You don't let anyone put anything past you. You fight to prove yourself to the gang. You don't smoke or drink because everyone else does; you do it because you want to. You do what you want, when you want. When somebody tries to make you do something you don't want to do, you fight back. You're usually a conservative in politics and you wonder what is going to happen to this country.

### School world

Finally, there is my school world. You are familiar with it, so I won't go into detail. I will only say I began to slip in my grades at the end of last year. I guess the newness and fear wore off. Now school tends to be a drag. Maybe going out for some activity would help. (I don't belong to any now.)

4

Well, that takes care of my four worlds and some of my problems and challenges. It is not exactly pretty, but it's honest. Would
you say I'm a successful teen-ager? A typical teen-ager?

4 How would you answer the
boy's question? Is he typical?
Successful? Explain. Describe
your four worlds.

# CHAPTER 2

# HOME WORLD

Nancy Konesko in "Is the Teen-
Swap for You?" describes a proposal to solve home problems.

### 3 TEEN-AGER TO TRADE

The ad really makes you stop and think: "Teen-ager to trade.
Have 14-year-old boy who wants to try different environment.
Would like to trade for teen-age boy or girl for one year."

It so happens that I have a 14-year-old son that I'd <u>give</u> away
at times, but could my husband and I really part with him for a
year? Could any parent really "swap" teen-agers as this Michigan
research scientist, J. D. Williams, has suggested?

Suppose that I did answer the ad, inserted in <u>Humanist</u> <u>Maga-</u>
<u>zine</u>, and traded my teen-age Michael for Mr. Williams' teen-
age Brian. How much more objective I could be with Brian, seeing him as another human being, rather than a part of myself.
In medieval times, knights usually traded sons and daughters for
this very reason.

Advantages?

What reader of the comic strip "Prince Valiant" can forget that
poignant scene when Valiant's son Arn was sent to live with another
family? Arn, impatient to start the adventure, Aleta fighting back
the tears while Val gave fatherly advice to which Arn obviously
wasn't listening.

Thus we see that nothing has changed these last few hundred

years. But say that Brian did come to live with us: If he were failing algebra through neglect of his homework, we would feel no qualms about turning off his television, and inspecting his finished papers. His soft brown eyes wouldn't remind me of my husband's, and thus melt my resistance. Indeed, we would feel honor-bound to help Brian improve his marks, knowing that Mr. and Mrs. Williams were doing the same for our Michael. We would, in a sense, be teaching the boys to joust with life in life's own terms.

More fair?

On the other hand, if Brian couldn't turn out a decent project in woodworking class, we would not have to ask ourselves "Where have we failed?" Three generations of our family have been outstanding carpenters--why must our son have two left thumbs?"

Instead, we could be objective. My husband would simply have a very adult discussion with our charge. "Brian, old man, you aren't going to swing it in carpentry. Why don't you consider the wrecking business? You'd be a natural for it."

We could be more fair with Brian in matters of discipline. We would feel compelled to say why he couldn't do a certain thing instead of taking the easy way out by screaming, "Because we're the parents, that's why!"

If Brian's manners occasionally slipped, we would not feel that it was a personal reflection on us and his earlier training. We could correct him in some kind, discreet way and he would listen and learn. Children always listen to outsiders, whereas with parents, they turn off a hidden device which closes their young minds and fixes a polite stare on their faces.

5 Would you agree that children listen more to outsiders than they do to their parents? Explain.

Different

. . . The point of all this is that not only would the children learn to cope with a different environment, different personalities, different rules, but the parents would also. In learning to deal with Brian as a person, I would be learning to deal with my own son the same way.

If nothing else, we would be so happy to see our son at the end of the year that we would appreciate him. Remember the return of Valiant's son? Val and Aleta set aside all else to listen to Arn's adventures. In his absence, they'd lost a little of their hold over him, and vice versa. . . .

But Arn learned to appreciate his parents as fellow human beings and even seemed to listen to them. Perhaps it is with this hope that parents across the nation have answered the Williams' ad. The Williams family is now setting up a clearing agency, the American Youth Exchange, to arrange similar trade for other teen-agers and their families.

. . . It would be interesting to see the results of test cases, a year from now. In this fast-changing world, a change of environment might be the very thing a child needs, occasionally to better understand himself and his place in the world.

6 What is good/bad about the teen-swap idea? Does it meet or avoid the home challenge facing parents and teen-agers? Why would you want/not want to be swapped?

## 4  WANTED: TRUST

I had a job at a drugstore, and everything was going nicely.
My parents were trusting me, and I could do almost anything I
wanted to do. Then something happened. I was fired from the
drugstore for stealing money from the registers.

The reason I did this is because I was getting 75¢ an hour,
which is pretty bad for a job like that. So I took after everybody
else and started stealing. Well, I got caught, and was fired. The
owner called my parents and told them. I got killed and they
won't trust me anymore.

So, like an immature baby, I had to get revenge on the owner
for firing me. On Halloween night, Rick Thompson (my house
guest for the weekend) and I went and put shaving cream and eggs
all over the guy's car. With my luck, the cops caught us. They
made us wash the car, and then took us home. I finally realized
how immature I had been and was ready to stop all this junk.

My problem is that now I can't get my parents to believe me
and get them to trust me again. I don't know. I just don't feel
like I belong if I am not trusted. I want to change. I want to be
trusted again. In other words, I want to turn over a new leaf.
But how do I go about it?

7  What can the boy do to get his
parents to trust him again?

10

In "Father Conroy Talks to Youth"
a worried mother seeks help to
solve a delicate problem.

## 5  NO COMMUNICATION

Dear Father Conroy:

We have a problem which, I think, is the problem of many other parents these days. I found some pictures of nude women in
the pockets of my 15-year-old son's trousers about three weeks
ago. To this day I don't know how to approach the matter of talking to him about it. I do not know where to begin. He is a good boy,
gets good grades and is wonderful to his younger sisters and
brothers. We thought we had brought him up in the right way,
but now this.

His father refuses to face the question at all, because he too
is crushed.

The boy knows we have found the literature and is terribly
embarrassed. How can we break this dilemma? What should
we say? What should we do? I know we have to do something.
This situation is getting unbearable.

8  How would you suggest that
the mother break this communication dilemma? Why do you
think the boy had the pictures?

## 6 SHORT FUSE

My mother always seems to be interested in what is going on
at school. Whenever I come home, she starts asking me questions.
One day while I was relaxing, she started to quiz me. I didn't
particularly want to be disturbed, so I answered her quickly and
a little disrespectfully. When my father heard the tone of my
voice, he corrected me instantly. I got a little upset and explained
to him why I used the tone. He listened, but didn't accept my explanation.

I suppose it is part of my mother's human nature to always
ask so many questions. I was tired, however, and didn't really
want to be bothered. That was probably the reason I had such a
short fuse. If I would have explained to her how I felt, she would
have understood. My father was right in telling me to be more
respectful. If I had used my head instead of flying off like that,
the incident would probably never have happened in the first place.
The next time something like this happens, I will think before I
say anything.

9 Why are mothers, especially, so curious about everything
her son or daughter does? How
would you handle the problem?

12

A junior reflects upon his inability to communicate easily.

## 7 I'M FIFTEEN

Another quiet evening in our household. Mom's come home
from work and fixed the dinner. Dad has gone to bed early after
his usual ten-hour day at the office. And I've completed this
evening's homework assignments. That's all I've done. I didn't
set the table. I didn't help with the dishes. I barely spoke to my
parents.

I'm fifteen, Lord, and I suddenly find myself too self-centered
to acknowledge my love for my parents. I realize how much this
admission would mean to them, still I hesitate to tell them how
much I love them. I can no longer easily express my appreciation
and wholehearted admiration.

Lord, give me the maturity required for straightforward relationships with my parents. I really love them, though I rarely
say so.

". . . you know that I really love you." John 21:15.

10 Is this student's problem
common to most teen-agers?
Why is it hard to express one's
feelings, especially to parents?

## 8 CONFLICT

A student describes a communication hang-up: the argument.

It started with my mother suggesting that I go to the barber,
which really isn't so earthshaking. I shrugged and intended to go
later in the day, perhaps after school. She took it as an act of resistance, for she suddenly got quite angry, shouting that I looked
like a dust mop. I said (or shouted) something at her; I can't remember what I said. She immediately began harping about some
other things--that I was sloppy, my bed wasn't made, that I was
always late. I got angry, for I was still half asleep, and didn't
want any shouting now.

I ate quickly, got my books for school, and stomped out of the
house.

Well, it turned out that this argument didn't really do anything
except to get my mother and myself pretty excited. She came back
from work later in the day. I came back from school, and we both
acted as if nothing had happened.

The only real thing this accomplished, outside of making me
remember about the haircut, was that both my mother and myself
let off a little steam.

11 Why do arguments usually
start with one subject but spread
to others? Do arguments usually
help or hurt a relationship?

14

## 9 STAY COOL

"Can I go to the Burger King after the movie tonight?" John asked his mother.

"The Burger King? You should be glad your Father and I let you go to the movies as often as we do during the school year."

"What d'ya mean? I don't see half as many movies as most kids my age do. I don't think you and Dad realize how strict you are about things like that," shouted John (throwing his hands in the air). "You're more like policemen than my parents! I don't think you trust me. If you don't believe me, ask her (pointing at his sister)."

### Raging inferno

Starting an argument with your parents is like tossing a lighted match into a dry haystack. It can get out of control and blaze out into a raging inferno before you know it.

Arguments are inevitable. They are bound to happen when people live close together. Arguments, however, should not strain or destroy a close relationship. Rather, they should strengthen it. A doctor will tell you that a broken bone, when healed, is stronger at the point of the break than it was before the break. The same thing should hold true of family squabbles.

A verbal war is meaningless if the two people involved end up

16

with no better understanding of each other than they did before it started. If an argument is to be useful, both parties should grow as a result of the discussion.

The first rule in arguing is to stick to the subject. In the above example, John and his mother are already off the subject. They have left the Burger King question and are on to something else: discipline and trust.

The second rule is not to call each other names or to accuse the other. When John implied that his mother was a policeman and accused her of not trusting him, he ceased to be objective and became subjective and unduly emotional.

The third rule is not to shout or engage in corny dramatics. When John raised his voice and threw up his hands, it was a sure sign that he was letting his emotions take over. Emotion is good at times, but when emotion replaces reason you're in trouble. Emotion is blind; reason alone is capable of vision. To allow the two to get reversed is like letting a blind dog lead around a seeing-eye man. It's just the opposite of what should be.

The fourth rule is not to leap to false conclusions. When John accuses his parents of not trusting him, he is jumping to a conclusion--which may or may not be true. The reason why his parents are so strict may be because they care about him. Parents are normally not sadistic. Most parents, who are strict, are that way because they care about their children. They value them. If they didn't, they wouldn't bother with them.

The fifth rule is to keep outsiders out. Audience participation is great, but not in an argument. When John suggested asking his sister, he was in danger of adding fuel to the fire. He was inviting a free for all. True, an outsider can sometimes be more objective, because he/she is not emotionally involved. But if you agree to submit your dispute to arbitration, agree beforehand to stick by the decision of the arbitrator.

When the argument is over, you should examine yourself on a few points. First, did I try to see the other person's side of the argument? Or didn't I even make an effort to consider it?

Second, was the argument really worth it? Or were we arguing about a trivial point that didn't matter in the long run? If it was a small point, why did we let ourselves get carried away by it? Was it because we were both edgy and irritable before we even began?

Third, did we settle the argument? If not, am I going to let it simmer and bubble within me the rest of the night? Am I going to hold a grudge, or store it up as ammunition for the next time we battle over some point?

Fourth, did we at least fight fair? If not, why not? If you did, chances are that you have both grown in understanding and respect for each other as a result of it.

12 Which rule do you break most in arguments? What should you do if the other person doesn't fight fair? If you have refuted all points, what should you do if they still won't give in?

A student replays an argument
he had recently with his father.

## 10 THINKING IT OVER

My dad and I were arguing about some trivial point. Halfway through the quarrel I realized that he was probably right. Not to lose face, however, I kept throwing in new angles and ideas. Before long the dialogue got so heated that both of us stomped off to different parts of the house.

Because of my stubbornness and pride, a rift had developed between us. Soon my temper cooled, and I admitted to myself that I was wrong. I should have kept my pride in check and not become so angry as to offend my father.

Open my eyes, Lord, to both sides of any situation. Let me not be blinded by my feelings. Help me to respect the ideas of others--even when I think mine are better.

"Children, yield obedience in the Lord to your parents, for that is right." Ephesians 6:1.

13 Is stubbornness the main reason why people won't give up in an argument? Over what topics do you usually argue with your parents? Why?

## 11 KNOW YOURSELF

The desire to express yourself
is a sign of personal growth.

What's causing the communication problem
you are now experiencing with your parents?
Whose fault is it--yours or theirs? If Christ
were a teen-ager today, would he also experience a communication problem with his
parents?

Surprisingly enough the answer to this
question is "yes."

Recall when Jesus went with his parents
to Jerusalem to celebrate the Jewish pass-
over. After the celebration, which went for
several days, Mary started back to Nazareth
with the women; Joseph with the men--as was
the custom in those days.

Due to a mix-up (you might call it a communication problem), each thought that Jesus
was in the company of the other. When the
mistake was finally discovered, Mary and
Joseph hurried back to Jerusalem. There
they found Jesus in the temple.

His mother said to him:
"Child, why did you behave

toward us in this way?
Oh, our hearts were heavy--
your father's and mine--
as we searched for you!"
He said to them:
"Why did you search for me?
I had to answer my Father's call,
and did you not know it?"
But they did not grasp the meaning
of the reply he made to them. Luke 2:48-50.

## Clue

Jesus' answer to his parents provides the clue to what is taking place in your own life. You are now entering adulthood. You are beginning to feel the urge to be about your Father's business. You are being called to assume a more responsible role in life. It is this call that you are now beginning to experience in a fuzzy but definite way. You are starting to cross the bridge into adulthood.

## Two-way growth

Concretely, you are going through a two-way growth. The first way is clear. You are growing up physically. You are getting taller and more attractive. Your body is growing stronger and developing.

But you are also growing in a second way--a more important way. You are growing spiritually--in courage, independence, and knowledge. This explains why you now want to make your own decisions and choices.

## No accident

It is no accident that you are growing in both ways at the same time. How so? Physically you are almost an adult. Your whole body has changed. You are now physically capable of bringing your own family into the world. But it takes more than physical power to be a parent. You need spiritual powers, too. For once your family comes, you must be able to guide it and protect it. This takes independent thinking, quick acting, and courage. Thus, along with your physical growth, God helps you to grow spiritually. He is helping you to develop a spirit of independent thinking and acting.

## Change

Just as one can go through an awkward stage physically, because his reach and step are undergoing rapid change, so too one can go through an awkward stage spiritually. This could be the reason for the trouble you are now experiencing with your parents.

Your desire for independence can get out of hand at times. You can be tempted to fly off the handle or to jump into a situation without seeing the whole picture. Here is where parents come in. They act as checks and guides to help you, to guide you, and to keep you from making mistakes that you might later regret. Thus, it may appear, at times, that your parents are holding you back. You may even mistake their action as a sudden change of attitude or lack of trust toward you.

14 In your own words explain: 1) the two-way growth you are now going through, 2) how you are experiencing an awkward stage in your spiritual growth.

## What to do?

The key to handling the problem is to realize what is happening within you. You are going through a period of change. You are in a period of important transition. You and your parents must both understand and accept this. You cannot control the behavior of your parents, but you can control your own behavior. As far as you are concerned, you must be patient with yourself and with your parents. You must make a special effort to get your parents' point of view. This will not be easy, but it will help you in your growth toward maturity and complete independence.

## Guide

The surest guide during this period of growth and transition is Christ, himself. He left us his own example.

The Bible ends the account of the finding in the temple with these words. "He [Jesus] then went down in their company and came to Nazareth, where he was subject to them. . . . and Jesus made steady progress, proportionately to his age, in understanding and in favor with God and men." Luke 2:51-52.

Like Christ, you should be subject to your parents. This does not mean that you will not have arguments or heated discussions with them at times. These are inevitable. It does mean, however, that you will love, honor, and respect them in a special way.

## Maturity

Normally, the obligation to love, honor, and respect parents is not too hard to carry out, because mothers and fathers are so worthy of it. There are times, however, when this will not be the case. For example, a father can be cruel to his children and to their mother. So, too, a mother can be unfaithful to her family or to her husband. Even here, however, children are obliged to retain a special regard for their parents. Children must be ready to forgive delinquent parents, as parents are ready to forgive delinquent children.

In his book, A Boy Grows Up, H. C. McKown makes this observation. Though it is addressed to boys, it applies to girls as well.

> A boy should begin to face the difficulties in this life by telling himself that no matter how good his intentions may be he cannot fix up everything and make it perfect. No family or school life is perfectly smooth and ideal. No parents or friends or teachers are always fair or reasonable or good-humored. . . . The person who cannot be happy unless everything is arranged exactly to suit him is not very grown up.

## Huckleberry humor

Finally, we might keep in mind the words of Samuel Clemens, who was not exactly a conformist. Anyone who has read his life can tell you that.

Writing under the name Mark Twain, he gave American literature a new maturity. Before him, most American writers modeled themselves after European writers. Twain broke with this pattern and drew upon the American scene for inspiration and style. Among Twain's works are Huckleberry Finn, Tom Sawyer, and Life on the Mississippi.

Twain is best known for his humor, but beneath his humor often lay a wealth of down-to-earth wisdom. Reflecting on his own problems with his parents, he wrote:

24

When I was a boy of fourteen, my father was so ignorant I could hardly stand to have the old man around. But when I got to be twenty-one, I was astonished at how much the old man had learned in seven years.

15 Explain Twain's remark. Do young people expect too much perfection in adults? How can you love and respect a delinquent parent? Isn't this unfair or, at least, unrealistic?

## 12 THE KID

Author Patrick Strickler in "Another Afternoon" makes us think about life and maturity.

A bird sang in a distant treetop as the kid walked down the street looking at the sidewalk. He carried a pile of San Francisco newspapers under his arm. He wanted to go to San Francisco and the papers were so he could read the classified ads for jobs. And read about San Francisco. He walked past City Hall and looked down the alley at the big white light bulb on which was printed "Police Department." Traffic went the other way on the one-way street. The kid crossed the street, walked on, and still had another block and a half to go to where his car was parked. He walked toward the car with the newspapers and his dream under his arm.

He thought as he walked: on such a nice, warm afternoon in the summer, me just a kid (at heart) walking down the street with my dream, and, maybe a big truck will pull into this driveway as I cross it and hit me, kill me, and knock the damned newspapers all over and the wind will pick them up; and then, then after I am dead, everybody will wonder what was he carrying a bunch of San Francisco newspapers around with him for.

That, he thought, is tragedy. He imagined the men at the newspaper office finding out that he had taken the San Francisco newspapers from the News office, and that he (the obituary writer) had been carrying them home under his arm. What a dreamer, they would say, just a kid.

But he reached his car safely and drove home without having an accident. He went into his house, piled the newspapers in a corner of his bedroom, and then he changed his clothes. He took off his light-weight summer suit and put on a khaki shirt and a khaki pair of pants. He slipped into clean sweat socks and put his ankle-high sneakers on. He laced them all the way up, sitting on the edge of his bed, one knee at a time tucked up under his chin as he laced.

His mother was fixing dinner for him, but he told her that he was not hungry. He said to her as he went out of the house (for the last time perhaps; who knew?) that he was going fishing down by the river. She said something to him as he went out.

### Age and maturity

On the drive to the river, with dusk drawing closer and the trees looking heavy in midsummer like overripe pregnant women, and the day's dust settling slightly, he was struck again with the thought that always held a peculiar power over him. It was the idea of land and its strength, its endurance, its age. Perhaps, because he had so little he was told, its maturity too. Sometimes he wanted to stretch out right downtown on the sidewalk and let the heat from the cement feed into him, baking him with the strange, unnamed power he felt the land had. But he didn't dare. It would be a foolish thing to do. Foolish looking. He wanted to stand naked in a big lake in the moonlight with his (dreamed-of) lover and let the waves pound coldly against them. But he had no lover.

Remembering a dog he had once, he told himself, as he got ready to cast a lure into the river, he wanted to live more than he wanted not to live. He had had a dog but he kicked it once too often and it went away. The lure was a fabulous bass-catcher which the manufacturer had taken out of production; it shot out over the water and fell into the current. He reeled in and nothing happened. He cast again. And again. Nothing. It came in without a hitch. No bass leaped out of hiding at the last second to take a swipe at the lure. It came in time after time, cast after cast, without a hitch. Not even a snag. He began to think: nothing ever happens.

### The great fish

The kid decided to stop using artificial lures. He took out a night-crawler harness which his uncle had taught him how to tie

before he died suddenly two summers before. He cast a huge
night crawler into the middle of the river. Carried deep into the
water by three sinkers, it struck a fish. The fish grabbed the
worm and thereby hooked itself. The kid was onto a fish. He
raced along the riverbank fighting with all his might for the first
few minutes. (Tirelessly, he remembered to think, like Santiago
and the Great Fish.) His wrist began to ache. Then the fish became a big bore; a heavy, big bore. He remembered men who
had hooked and landed bigger fish than this, and in harder times,
too. He renewed the fight. The rod bent. Finally the big fish
turned. It dropped its head. It flopped. It was just a big fish
dying.

The kid readied his net for the fish. But the net was too small
and the fish was too big. He looked closely at the fish: its scales
are big and gray, overlapping like a bunch of toenails--soft and
ugly--and the fish is only a carp, although a big carp. He cut the
line and gave up his fishing.

The kid drove away from the river remembering many things
in the twilight. Men whose lives had been wasted (perhaps);
leaves burning, and big fish (a mixture in his mind of things
and ideas and men); and all the lost things he should have pocket-
ed and kept when he was a kid, and put in his mind, too. But
he was no longer a kid, he remembered sadly, and he decided
to throw out the San Francisco newspapers.

> 16  What is the point of this short
> story? What parts of it struck
> you most? How does it apply to
> you?

## 13 SELF-DISCOVERY

A high-school junior thinks about
what it means to be mature.

"Unless the grain of wheat falls into the ground and dies, it
remains alone. But if it dies, it brings forth much fruit. He who
loves his life, loses it; and he who hates his life in this world,
keeps it unto life everlasting." John 12:24-25.

Christ's words are packed with wisdom. But you have to dig
for it--just as you do for all treasures. Christ says we must give
ourselves if we are to find ourselves and grow to maturity. Love,
alone, will empower us to do this. And love begins at home. Without love, our lives are empty and powerless, like a flashlight without a battery. We find ourselves only when we give ourselves.

Help us, Lord, to give of ourselves--to love. Help us to think
less about ourselves and more about others. You, who are love,
show us the meaning and power of love.

"Let us not love in word . . . but in deed and in truth." 1 John 3:18.

17 Explain: "he who hates his
life." What does it mean to "accept" yourself? Do teen-agers,
in general, accept themselves?
Explain.

## 14 EXPRESSING YOURSELF

Problems in communication
can lead to other problems.

Someone once said, "If I had to give up everything I own except one thing, I would keep my power of speech, because with it I could get everything back again."

New words invade our language daily. Since the time of Shakespeare, for example, 140,000 new English words have entered our vocabulary--increasing it to approximately 750,000 words. Teddy Roosevelt would probably have to take a refresher course in word study to make sense out of the daily paper. He never heard of such words or expressions as: atomic bomb, countdown, babysitter, contact lenses, flying saucers, microfilm, smog, parking meter, or uncola.

18 Name at least ten other words that Roosevelt wouldn't understand if he picked up the daily newspaper today.

Word power

The gift of speech is man's most powerful possession. Words can be used to help or to hurt. As Time magazine put it, "Ambassadors have no battleships at their disposal, or heavy infantry or fortresses. Their weapons are words and opportunities."

A University of Arkansas professor estimates that the talkative American utters an average of 30,000 words per day. It would be interesting if another university professor would do some research to determine how many of these words are used to hurt people. A Look magazine editorial put it well when it said:

> They sing. They hurt. They teach. They sanctify. They are man's first immeasurable feat of magic. They liberate us from ignorance and our barbarous past. For without these marvelous scribbles which build letters into words, words into sentences, sentences into systems and sciences and creeds, man would be forever confined to the self-isolated prison of the scuttlefish or the chimpanzee.

### Vehicles and mirrors

Words are man's vehicle of communication. He can use them either to confuse or to clarify, to teach or to tear down, to promote peace or to stir up unrest.

But when one delves more deeply into the mystery of words, he begins to realize that our words are only the conveyor belts of our thoughts. They are mirrors of what we think and how we think. Our thought life really determines what words we use and how we use them.

### The key

Learning to think clearly and logically is the key to better communication. It is also the key to a better world and a better home and school life.

How many accusations, how many arguments, how many uncharitable thoughts stem from faulty or illogical thinking? Take a few examples of how people think illogically.

He defends demonstrations and lock-ins, therefore he is a communist. He criticizes black agitation, therefore he is a bigot. He burns his draft card, therefore he is a coward or unpatriotic. His parents believe in discipline, therefore they are old-fashioned and out of it. He has long hair, sideburns, and tight pants, therefore he is a young bum.

19 What is wrong with this kind of thinking? Why do people engage in it so frequently?

## Lice and cigarettes

Besides leaping to false conclusions by generalizing from a
particular, we can also leap to false conclusions by other ways.
For example, when one event precedes another in time, we tend
to conclude the first event caused the second. We are like the
rooster who is positive that his crow at dawn makes the sun come
up. He observes that after he crows, the sun always appears. A
few examples will illustrate this.

Natives of certain islands in the South Pacific believe that lice
keep people healthy. They draw this conclusion because they
observe that many healthy people have lice, which the sick do not
always have. The real explanation is quite different. When a man
gets sick in that tropical climate, he frequently runs a fever. Lice
do not like it that hot and leave.

## Other examples

The historian Gibbon observed that Christianity rose about
the same time that the Roman Empire hit the skids. He concluded
that Christianity helped to destroy Rome. No historian today would
endorse such a conclusion.

Statistics show that college students who smoke get lower
grades than those who do not. People who don't approve of smoking
use these figures to prove that smoking leads to poor scholarship. In reality, the same figures might be used to prove just the
reverse: poor scholarship leads a student to take up smoking.

## Half animal

Another way of leaping to a false conclusion is by equating
two things that should not be equated. Such a person might reason this way: "A square has four sides. This rectangle has four
sides. Therefore it is a square."

Or a person might reason this way: "Animals have four legs.
John has two legs. Therefore John is not an animal." The person might just as well have reasoned this way: "Animals have
four legs. John has two legs. Therefore John is half animal."

Ridiculous as it may seem, this kind of reasoning goes on
frequently. Next time you watch TV commercials or hear a bigot
hold forth, be on the lookout for it. But more important, ask yourself this question: "Am I hurting people by accusing them or
judging them rashly by this kind of faulty reasoning?"

20 Point out some of the false
conclusions that TV commercials
try to get people to make. Is it
morally wrong to try to deceive
people in this way?

## 15 WRONG

A senior describes how easy it
is to misjudge other people.

Recently I was able to see how easy it is to make rash judgments
about the character of others. I was lucky enough to be nominated
for a scholarship by a man whom I had thought to be a biased indi-
vidual--biased against me. I was filled with resentment against
him for imagined wrongs.

But when he honored me in this way, I saw how wrongly I had
judged him. My own prejudice against him was at fault; I had let
my feelings obscure the facts.

Help me, Lord, not to judge others rashly. Help me to take
into account all the facts. Help me to see that I often judge only
on the surface, not in depth. I must not make generalizations
which do not apply.

"Judge not by appearances but give just judgment." John 7:24.

21 Give examples of generalizations that do not apply. What
is circumstantial evidence? How
else can you judge, if not by appearances?

## 16 DO IT WITH STYLE

The way you communicate
marks you as a person.

Communication is an art.
Some people are amateurs at
it. Others have style. Knowing the art is the key to style.

Communication usually takes
the form of discussion, debate,
argument, or dialogue. Often it
mixes up these four forms.

We have already explored

some of the differences between discussion and argument. Discussion aims at exchanging ideas in a reasonable way. It usually follows certain informal rules and procedures. A discussion degenerates into an argument when the parties involved become subjective and emotional, when they engage in accusations, name-calling, and exaggerated dramatics.

Debate and dialogue are closely related to discussion, but have different aims. The aim of a debate is to defeat an opponent. A debate is a contest in wits. The purpose of debating is to triumph over your opponent.

Dialogue, on the other hand, has a completely different aim. Its purpose is to help all parties involved to come closer to the truth. It is a kind of heart-to-heart talk in which our genuine concern for the other persons (even though we disagree with what they say) surpasses our desire to triumph over them.

John Mahoney puts it well when he says, "In true dialogue, we will not try to ram an idea through with a barrage of authorities or statistics. We would not claim excessive deference to our status as experts, as if no one else had the right to hold a view. . . . The whole bundle of clever debate tactics would count against, not for their user. We would not try to prevent an opponent from being heard, or from making the best statement of his case; we would help him do both."

22 How does the way you communicate mark you as a person? What form of communication should a religion class take?

## 17 NOBODY CARES

A high-school student spotlights
another communication hang-up.

Our class was discussing a point in religion. One of the students
was trying desperately to speak above the murmurings of his fellow
classmates. Finally, he said, "Oh, what's the use. You people don't
care. You're not listening."

Whether in school or at home, we are constantly drawn into
discussion, forced to communicate our opinions and to listen to
the ideas of others. Many of us are so caught up in our own point
of view and importance that we forget that the purpose of communication is to share and learn. We are often so bent on putting
forth our own opinions that we ignore the insights of others.

Help me, God, to remember that an important goal of commu-
nication--like one of the important goals in life--is to cooperate
and to share with others.

"He who listens to advice is wise." Proverbs 12:15.

23 Why are some students
tuned out by the class almost
before they start speaking?
How can this situation be rem-
edied?

More and more, films are being used to communicate ideas and to spark discussion among people. Sometimes film presentations are clear and to the point. At other times, they can leave us wondering, "Now what was that all about." It is not uncommon to hear someone say, "That film was stupid. It had no plot. It didn't communicate a thing to me."

This comment brings out an important point that many people miss. Not every film is supposed to have a plot. Films are similar to discussions; they have different purposes. Just as the form a discussion takes will vary according to its purpose, so does the form of a film vary in the same way.

### Four forms

There are four common film forms: 1) story, 2) survey, 3) symbol, 4) sensitivity.

A <u>story</u> film is simply a film that tells a story. It has a plot. Most commercial movies and TV stories fall into this category.

A <u>survey</u> film is a documentary. It reports or surveys a life or world situation. An example would be "The Tenement" which surveys the wretched living conditions of a big city ghetto. Most TV Special Reports fall into this category. They merely inform us about a current life situation, such as slums, drugs, or campus unrest.

A symbol film is one which uses symbols to get across its message. An example would be "The Parable," "The Supper," or "It's About This Carpenter." Thus "The Parable" is not just a film about a circus clown. It has a far different purpose and a far deeper meaning. So, too, "The Supper" is not just a story about a man who doesn't want to be bothered. It, too, has a deeper message. The same holds true for the carpenter who runs into all kinds of trouble trying to deliver the cross he has made for a church. Symbol films are like Christ's parables. They have a deeper meaning than the one that appears on the surface.

A sensitivity film is one which tries to awaken in the viewer a realization of some aspect of life. An example would be "The Universe." It tries to sensitize the viewer to the immensity of creation. That is, it tries to make us realize or appreciate in a new way something we have always taken for granted.

Naturally, some films overlap these four categories. "The Universe" both surveys outerspace and sensitizes us to its immensity.

## Discussing films

The first step in discussing a film is to decide whether it is a story, survey, symbol, or sensitivity film--or a combination of these four. The first step is a question of film identification. Recall that this is the same procedure we follow in reading the Bible. We ask ourselves: "Is Christ narrating a true story, or is he merely telling a parable?" Until we decide this, we are in no position to understand what he is trying to get across to us. This leads us automatically to the second step.

The second step is to decide what point the film is trying to make. For example, if the point of the film "The Parable" is not to tell us about the adventures of a circus clown, what point is it trying to make? The second step is assimilation. Did we get the message?

The third step is to isolate and discuss those parts or points in the film that were either confusing or controversial. It is a question of clarification, that is, trying to clear up some point in the film that I either didn't understand or tended not to agree with. For example, in "The Parable" what was the point behind the scene where the clown takes the place of the black man sitting above the tank of water?

The fourth step is to probe the relevancy of the film. How does

40

it apply to a young person's life today? The fourth step is a question of <u>application</u> to one's life. For example, how does the point made in "The Parable" apply to me personally?

Naturally, a film discussion--or any discussion--must have freedom and flexibility. On the other hand, too often discussions become aimless and endless. Some order and direction are needed. The above steps are merely one way of achieving this.

24  List some recent films you have seen. How would you classify them? What are the advantages of a film over a book? Vice versa? Do you think films and TV will ever replace books and newspapers?

*We may not give our words a second thought, but other people do.*

## 19 BLUE WORDS

Today our state department and many big business firms hire people who do nothing but listen to conversations. These people are engaged in a new technique called, "content analysis." This means they monitor broadcasts of other nations and read reports and press releases of other firms for small verbal clues which appear meaningless in themselves, but when put together, yield valuable information.

Thus a government or a business firm can detect political or competitive strategies before they go into effect. Frequent words or phrases are one of the surest clues to finding out what another is thinking--or planning.

For example, when a girl goes for weeks without mentioning the name Mike, and then begins to mention it in every conversation, you know what is taking place in her mind and her heart.

So, too, when the topic of conversation in the school lunchroom switches from one TV show to another, you know which show is on the way in and which is on the way out with young viewers.

25 In your own words, explain the idea behind content analysis. Explain how the political or religious leanings of a newspaper are reflected in its news copy.

Spontaneous

The words we use to express sudden anger, joy, or disappointment are usually spontaneous and unreflective. We use them without thinking. They just come out. Because of this, some experts say that these unreflective words serve as clues or insights into the type of personality that we are unconsciously developing.

For example, if our spontaneous words are coarse, then perhaps our personality is tending in that direction too. We may not give a second thought to this, but other people do. What do they think about it?

Here is what sophomore girls in a midwestern high school think of a boy who unthinkingly--or thinkingly--uses profanity in their presence.

Nancy: Profanity bothers me. I certainly don't think he's more of a man when using it. I rather think he's a little boy trying to grow up, but not knowing how. If a guy respects a girl, he won't use profanity in front of her.

Madge: It doesn't impress me when a boy uses profanity, because anyone can say things. You can teach a bird to swear. It doesn't prove a thing. But on the other hand, it doesn't turn me off. I really don't mind it that much.

Rita: When a boy uses profanity around girls, it doesn't really bother me. Why get excited? Words are only words.

Cathy: It bothers me rather than impresses me. I've heard all the four-letter words since I was a kid in grade school. The only thing I can say is that there is a time and a place for everything. It's just showing your stupidity and lack of vocabulary.

Shelly: It makes me feel that he has no respect for me. It's

44

like he regards me as just one of the guys. My boy friend doesn't swear in front of me, and if one of the other guys does it, he'll tell him to knock it off.

Pam: It neither impresses nor annoys me. I don't even know he's there. It's his hang-up apparently; and if that's the only way he can express himself--let him go right ahead.

> 26 Do most people use profanity thinkingly or unthinkingly? List the reasons why a person uses profanity.

## 20 FOR GIRLS ONLY!

Boys too have their opinions
about girls who use profanity.

Mike: Girls by nature are supposed to be dainty, feminine, ladylike. This is the way I prefer a girl to be. . . . A girl who uses profanity or swears really turns me off.

Tony: Girls who swear really don't affect me. That is girls I really don't care for. If I really cared for a girl--I mean really cared--and she swore a lot, I think I would tell her what I thought of her vocabulary.

Denny: It depends on what mood I'm in. If I'm out with the guys and we're looking for kicks, if you hear them swear, you've got a live one. But if you hear a good girl swear, it is sort of revolting.

Bill: I think that a girl who uses a word now and then--not every sentence or minute, is all right. It seems to emphasize the fact that nobody is perfect. . . . I feel that vulgar language is not bad, but a sign of bad taste.

Pete: It's a pity so many girls act so unfeminine. For example, last year I saw two girls with a group of idiots (guys) urging them on to fight in an alley! It was sickening! Two girls who'd have looked pretty if they acted more like their sex, actually fighting, kicking, and swearing.

Jack: I went to a bowling alley a few months ago, and a girl I knew introduced me to one of her friends. Well, she happened to be a girl--originally. I don't mean to be critical, but since

this requires my opinion, I'll be straight about it. Without the
ton of makeup that she obviously had on, I bet she had a pretty
good-looking face. She wore a boy's ring on her right finger,
and had a cigarette behind her ear. The words she used sounded
four times as bad because they came from a girl. It isn't right
for a girl to use these words. It's unfeminine. I might have liked
her once, but not the way she was now.

Gary:  If I were going with a girl who started to use profanity
regularly, I would: 1) feel she was being poorly brought up, 2) be
embarrassed to take her out with my friends, 3) drop her.

Pete:  For a long time now, women have been trying to become
equal to men--becoming doctors, lawyers, even joining youth
gangs. I think this is why girls swear. They want to be equal
with guys. Guys swear. Thus, in trying to be equal, they swear
too.

27  Do you agree with what
Pete just said?

## 21 PROFANITY FALLOUT

Why do people use profanity?
Here are some reasons they give.

One way to eliminate or control profanity fallout is to find out why and under what circumstances it usually occurs. Here is what some students have to say about when and why they sometimes use profanity.

1 To let off steam or to vent emotion. "Probably the main reason why I swear is that it lets off steam. When some people get mad, they might kick a piece of furniture, keep it bottled up inside them, do some push-ups, pray to God, do some physical labor, beat up someone, or get drunk. Me, I'm not so imaginative. I just swear. You notice, that out of the above reasons, my solution works best. It's the fastest, works in the least amount of time, and works best. Because of that they call it a problem."

2 Out of habit. "The only reason I use bad language is out of habit. I heard older boys use it when I was little. Though I didn't know what it meant then, I would repeat it to my friends. But I was always careful, for some reason, not to say it in front of my parents. . . . I know I probably can't stop it at this moment; but I don't intend to keep it up all my life. Vulgarity in an adult is kind of immature."

3 To joke. "I sometimes use profane or vulgar language out

48

of fun, usually when I am alone with some of my friends. . . .
Most of us realize it's not the best thing. People judge you by
your speech. Sloppy speech, if it's done a lot, is the sign of a
sloppy personality."

4  To stress a point. "I sometimes use profanity to stress
a point or give my speech more force. The pulpit-pounders
pound their fists to make a point. I verbally pound my fist to get
a point across. . . . Swearing is not bad, but if it is done too
much you defeat your purpose. You lose the shock effect that
you are trying to get."

5  To be "in" or cool. "Usually there is a pretty good reason
for my swearing. What I am saying is that not every word I
utter is a cuss word. Sometimes when I am with a group of tough
guys I swear. Sometimes I find that it's necessary, even with
some girls."

6  To cover up. "Many young people swear because of a limited vocabulary and stupidity. They get in an argument and become
outwitted. They feel like they are backed into a corner, and also
feel that they must save face. So they start swearing. They're
too dumb to realize that other people can't see this."

28  What other reasons would
you add? How widespread is
profanity around school? Is
habitual profanity a sign of
bad taste, immaturity, or
neither? Is it unchristian?

## 22 FREEDOM NOW

A sophomore raises the delicate
question of parental authority.

Recently my parents and I had an argument about where their
authority ended and my freedom began. Specifically, the argument was about the proper age to begin dating.

It really wasn't so much an argument as it was a heated debate.
My parents insisted that I was too young to date a girl. By this
they meant that it would not be safe for me to be alone with a
girl on a date at my age.

I asked my father if he trusted me. He said that he did. So
then I said that if the boy is at a reasonable age, the decision
should be left partly up to him also. Because if a boy feels he
is mature enough to date alone, then he should be allowed to do so.

I usually don't have much trouble with my parents because they
are such good people. But, I think, this question of dating is one that
should be settled.

29  What is the reasonable age for
a boy/girl to begin dating? Who
should have the last say when
a dispute arises, such as it did
in this boy's case? Explain.

## 23 TRUST

A junior reflects on the need for trust in the home world.

Last summer my parents took a vacation and left me alone in an eight-room house. I was completely on my own, free to run the house and my personal life. My parents placed their complete trust in me, and I had to prove--as never before--that I was worthy of that trust.

Through this experience I discovered the true relationship between freedom and responsibility.

Lord, help other sons and daughters become aware of the true meaning of this relationship. Help other parents have the courage to trust their sons and daughters--and realize how important this trust is in helping each mature.

"You shall know the truth, and the truth shall make you free." John 8:32.

30 Can parents place too much trust in their children? How should they decide how much trust to place in them? What is the relationship between freedom and responsibility?

I wanna be free like the wind,
laugh in the sun, and have fun.


## 24 ALL SYSTEMS "GO"

A crucial stage in every space flight is when the space vehicle
leaves one orbital system and enters another. The captain of the
space vehicle does not execute this operation alone. He is supported and assisted by a fantastic backup crew.

So, too, when the young adult leaves one orbit of life (childhood) and enters another (adulthood). He is in a crucial stage of his
flight to maturity. Like a space captain and a space vehicle, he
cannot execute this operation alone. He needs the support and assistance of a backup crew.

This brings up the whole question of freedom (young adult) and
authority (parents and teachers). How do the two function together so that true teamwork and harmony result?

### Born free?

A few years ago the song "Born Free" was breaking all kinds
of sales records. The song says we were born free like the blowing wind, the growing grass, and the roaring tide--we were born
free to follow the movement of our hearts. The song tells us to
live free and to stay free--life is worth living only because we
were born free.

A question arises: what is freedom? Is it the "ability to go
where we want to go, just as the wind blows where it wants to

blow"? Does it mean we are free to delight people as the wind delights the crew of a sailboat? And are we just as free to destroy homes and towns as the wind is free to destroy them?

> 31 How does your idea of free-
> dom square with the songwriter's
> idea of it?

Different slant

The Declaration of Independence does not speak of being born free, but rather of being born with the right to be free. This automatically raises a second question: are we born free, or are we born with the right to be free? What is the difference between the two?

> 32 How would you answer this
> latter question?

Unmixable?

About the same time that "Born Free" was sweeping the country, the Monkies sent record sales soaring with the song entitled, "I Wanna Be Free."

The song speaks of being free like the bluebird, the blue sea, and the September wind. The songwriter speaks of "laughing in the sun" and "having fun," but with no strings attached. He doesn't want to be loved, but only liked, because love would restrict his freedom. This raises still another question about freedom: are freedom and love like oil and water--unmixable?

> 33 How would you answer this
> third question about freedom?

## 25 FREEDOM

Let us now try to unscramble the idea of freedom. Freedom, like so many other things, comes in different varieties. It has several faces.

First there is what philosophers call <u>physical</u> freedom. This is the kind of freedom that a man enjoys if he is not physically restrained. Thus a man in handcuffs is not physically free. His movements are restrained or restricted.

### Power to choose

A second kind of freedom is called <u>natural</u> freedom. This freedom is peculiar to man and distinguishes him from the animal world. For example, a bird is not free to build a ranch style or a colonial nest. It can only build the type of nest that its instinct dictates. Man, on the other hand, is not tyrannized by such an instinct. By nature he has been given the power to choose the kind of home he will build.

### Real freedom

A third and even more important kind of freedom is what some philosophers call <u>personal</u> freedom. Even though man has the power to make decisions about his own life, he may not be free because of two big reasons.

First, he may not have the required knowledge that he needs to make a choice. For example, a person lost in a deep wilderness is not free with regard to returning to civilization or remaining in the wilderness. He is enslaved by his lack of knowledge on how to get out.

Second, even if a person has the required knowledge to make a choice, he still may lack the required virtue to choose freely. That is, he may allow his prejudice or passion to dominate him to such an extent that they enslave him.

For example, a person may know that he should treat all men as brothers, but his prejudice keeps him from doing this. Though he knows what is right, he lacks the necessary virtue to carry it out. He is a slave to prejudice.

Thus our most important freedom, personal freedom, is something that must be acquired. Without the necessary knowledge and the necessary virtue, a person is not truly free. He is a slave to his ignorance and his prejudice and/or passion.

> 34 Ray says, "How can I be sure I am not being influenced by my passions or prejudices?"

### Shocked

Prejudice explains why certain Jews refused to accept Christ in spite of his teaching and his miracles. They had their minds all made up about what God's kingdom should be like and what the promised Messiah should do. They thought God's kingdom should be a worldly one that would catapult Israel into first place among the nations. They also thought the Messiah should wear a crown of gold and not a crown of thorns. When Christ told them that his kingdom was not to be of this world and that he would suffer and die, they were shocked and angered. They did not want to hear this. It contradicted their own pet ideas about the kingdom and the Messiah. They refused to listen to reason. In other words, they allowed their personal feelings to blind them to truth.

Just as prejudice can enslave man, so can passion. If we allow our passions to dominate us, we actually become a slave to them. We allow our passions to keep us from following the path that we know we should follow. St. Paul referred to this when he said that he saw and approved of the better things, but he did the worse. Romans 7:15.

56

Without knowledge, man is a slave to his ignorance. So, too, a man without virtue is a slave to his passions and prejudices. Man is not born free. He is born with the power and the right to become free. Freedom is won. That is what maturity and personality development are all about.

35 Sheila says, "If passion robs me of my freedom, then I can't be responsible for what I do." Comment.

## Christ and freedom

In John 8:32 Christ said to the people, "You shall know the truth, and the truth shall make you free." Christ came to set man free in two ways: 1) from the chains of his ignorance, and 2) from the chains of his passions and prejudices.

First, Christ freed us from the chains of our ignorance by explaining to us the truths of this world and the next.

Second, Christ freed us from the chains of our passions and prejudices by instructing us and empowering us to love one another. For only love can wipe out jealousy and hate. Seen in this way, love does not stand in the way of freedom. Rather, it makes freedom possible.

## Recap

In brief, we see that there are three kinds of freedom: 1) physical, by which I am not physically restricted, 2) natural, by which I can make choices, and 3) personal, by which I have sufficient knowledge and sufficient virtue to keep my intellect and will from being enslaved by ignorance and by passion and prejudice.

Only by seeing freedom in this light can we understand what it means to be free. Without this understanding of freedom, we are doomed to flounder about in utter confusion.

It is especially important that every Christian understand what freedom is. Once he does, he discovers a whole new vision of himself and Christ's freeing role in his life. He understands St. Paul's words, "Christ has set us free." Galatians 5:1.

36 In what sense is the quest for freedom never ending?

## 26 FACES OF AUTHORITY

Now that we have a clearer picture of freedom, let us look at authority. Like freedom, it has several faces.

Today, the word <u>authority</u> is under a shadow. Some people look upon authority as a force restricting freedom, rather than making it possible.

Other people look upon authority as a club of the establishment, ever poised to come crashing down upon us. This view of authority is completely opposed to the way Christ viewed authority and intended it to be used.

### Freeing force

Authority may be compared to a gun. It all depends on how it is viewed and used. It can be an instrument of service, or it can be an instrument of destruction. Let us now center our attention on Christ's view of authority.

As we saw in the reading on freedom, Christ intended authority to act as a freeing force in man's search for happiness. For example, when an authority on pole vaulting instructs me on how to clear the bar, he is not bossing me or destroying my freedom by his instruction. True, he may give me his instructions in a bossy way, but that is beside the point. The point to be grasped is this. The instructor makes it possible for me to choose to participate in this sport or not. Before he taught me, I had no choice, because I did not know how to proceed. Only after he taught me, could I truly choose to engage in this sport or not.

In a similar way, a soldier lost in a jungle is not free to find his way out; he does not know which direction to take. Thus if he accidentally discovers a signpost on a footpath, the marker does not dictate to him or take away his freedom because it points out the direction for him. Rather it makes him free for the first time. He can now choose to stay in the jungle or not. Before he had no choice in the matter.

Authority, seen from this point of view, is really a liberating factor in man's life. By remedying a deficiency of knowledge in him, it serves to free man, not to restrict him. This liberating function of authority is sometimes called its remedial function.

> 37 Bob says, "I could learn to pole-vault by experimenting myself or by reading a book. I don't need any authority to tell me how to do it." Comment.

## Captain and team

Let us now focus our attention on yet another function of authority. We can illustrate in this way. Suppose our class organized a basketball team to compete in the school's intramural tournament. The first thing we would do is to elect a captain who would be responsible for the strategy we use. Clearly there could be much disagreement about the strategy we might employ. But if the team is to be successful, we will have to come to some sort of agreement on this point. It is the job of the captain to decide on one particular plan of action.

The captain's decision does not destroy the freedom of the other members of the team. Rather, it frees them to win. If every team member acted on his own, the team would never jell. It could never hope to win consistently.

The authority of the captain is needed to decide on the strategy to be used. His decision frees the team from confusion and unifies it. This function of authority is sometimes called its essential function.

> 38 Ann says, "A captain isn't really necessary. A team could decide by vote on what strategy to use." Comment.

## Dual need

When we understand the dual function of authority, we see that authority addresses itself to a twofold need in man's nature. By nature man is: 1) sin-scarred, and 2) social.

Man's nature is sin-scarred in the sense that, because of original sin, man's intellect and will are impaired. This means that, at times, he stands in need of instruction and guidance. It is to this aspect of man's nature that authority, first of all, addresses itself.

Man's nature is also social. No man is an island. Men live together, work together, have common problems, and pursue common goals. Thus men stand in need of some unifying force in their lives. Authority acts as this force.

Authority not only remedies man's fallen (sin-scarred) nature, but it also unifies and harmonizes his social nature. Authority thus frees men, individually and collectively, from error and confusion.

## Christ

Christ used his authority to free men individually and collectively. First, Christ explained the Scriptures to men; he taught them the meaning and purpose of life. By his teaching, Christ freed men. They were no longer slaves to ignorance about themselves or life. This is what Christ meant when he said, "You shall know the truth, and the truth shall make you free." John 8:32.

Christ's teaching does not restrict man; rather it frees him. The commandments are not roadblocks, but rather road signs to guide man in his search for freedom and happiness.

In a similar way, Christ used his teaching to unify man. His command to love our neighbor as ourselves was aimed at helping us to function as a team in working out our individual and collective salvations. The law of love welds us into a family or a people of God. It dissolves the jealousy and hate that tend to divide us. It enables all men of all races, colors, and creeds to work together toward their common goal: perfect love and happiness.

39 In your own words explain how Christ's teaching directs itself to: 1) man's sin-scarred nature, 2) man's social nature.

Authority is something precious. The purpose of authority is to serve man, not to restrict him. Unfortunately, those who exercise authority do not always use it properly. This was true in Christ's time (recall the Pharisees). It is still true today. Human nature has not changed.

Thus, though we must always respect authority, we have the right--even the duty--to challenge those leaders who misuse it. Unless we distinguish between: 1) the idea of authority, and 2) the person who exercises authority, we are in trouble.

Law, as Christ envisioned it, is also something precious. The purpose of law is to serve man, not to restrict him. It is to aid him in his search for happiness.

There are two kinds of laws: divine and human. Divine law comes from God--for example, the commandments. Human law, however, is man-made--for example, traffic laws or curfew laws.

Divine laws, because they come from God, are always just. Human laws, because they come from man, can sometimes be unjust. When a law is unjust, we have the right--even the duty-- to change it. This is why we have courts--to give us a means of objectively determining whether a law is just or not.

On the other hand, no man has a right to declare a divine law

unjust. It can happen, however, that there can be a question as
to whether or not a divine law applies in this or that situation.
For example, how does God's law forbidding the taking of another's life apply when it comes to protecting one's own life
against an enemy?

To help us in a situation like this, Christ has entrusted to his
Church the power of interpretation. Christ said to Peter, I will
give you the keys of the kingdom of heaven: what you prohibit on
earth will be prohibited in heaven; what you permit on earth
will be permitted in heaven (Matthew 16:18-19).

By giving Peter this power, Christ also gave him power to
make disciplinary laws to guide his followers.

### Two kinds

Just as laws, in general, fall into two divisions, so the laws
of the Church fall into two divisions.

First, there are the divine laws, which Christ gave us.

Second, there are the laws which the successors of Christ have
seen fit to make, to help us live out our Christian lives more effectively. These latter laws are sometimes called disciplinary
laws. Fast and abstinence regulations are an example of these
laws.

Divine laws can never be done away with or changed. Disciplinary laws, however, may be changed or done away with when
it becomes clear that they no longer sufficiently help a majority
of Christians to lead better Christian lives. This was the reason
many fasting laws were eliminated several years ago. They ceased
to be of helpful service to the majority of Christians.

40 What does it mean to distinguish between: 1) the idea
of authority, and 2) the person
who exercises it? Explain why
church disciplinary laws can
and should change from time
to time.

CHAPTER **3**

# PARISH WORLD

Father Henry in "What You Oughta
Do, Father . . ." describes some
of the modern pastor's problems.

## 28 PASTOR ON A TIGHTROPE

I'm the pastor of a fairly large city parish and I'd like to clue
you in. What I mean is: a lot of pastors are taking the rap these
days for either being too fast or too slow . . .

What started me on this train of thought was meeting one of my
seventh graders the other day. With shining face and innocent eye,
he looked up at me and what he said was:

"Father, you know what you oughta do?"

. . . "You oughta have a guitar Mass on Sunday. . . ."

My thoughts did a flashback to the previous Sunday as I stood
outside church after Mass. One of my redoubtable parishioners
(of female persuasion) approached me . . .

"You know what you should do, Father?"

. . . "You should see to it that every guitar in this city is burned
in its own lacquer. I hope you are not thinking of allowing anyone
to strum those noisy things in our church."

. . . Sometimes, sitting at my messy desk in a quiet moment, I
indulge in just a little self-pity. How does one go about pleasing
1000 human beings? . . .

41 To what extent should the
pastor try to please everybody?
Are guitars the answer to better youth participation at Mass?

## Other problems

There was Mr. K. who ambled up to me after Mass one Sunday.
. . . "It's too stuffy in church. You should turn down the heat and
open a few windows. Besides it would save us some money on
heat." So right after that Mrs. W. came out and said: "I froze
in church this morning. We surely aren't that poor. What you
ought to do is put up a little more gas."

There was Mr. L. . . . he said, "You should stop talking
about money. We are . . . giving all we can, and we like to hear
spiritual things when we come to Mass on Sunday." But at the
Holy Name meeting two days later, Mr. B. . . . suggested in
no uncertain terms: "There are a lot of people in our parish who
are not tithing and you should get up there and really give it to
them on Sunday." . . .

And so it goes: "Father, you should do more for our youth--
to keep them off our streets." "Father, you shouldn't let the
kids in our gym all the time. They are ruining it." Sometimes
I get twin suggestions like this: "Father, why don't you let a
board of laymen run the school. . . ." And the next day: "Father, you should run the school with an iron hand. Things are
too lax around here. When I was in school, kids didn't get away
with those things. Too many people have too much to say."

## What to do?

. . . What would you do if you were being pulled from both
sides like the rope in a tug-o-war? And both sides were getting
angry, and you liked both sides? One solution is to make a decision and then hide out in the boiler room where only the janitor
will know where you are. Or you can refuse to accept any calls
because you have the "flu," while one side says: "He's too modern,"
and the other side says: "He's an old fogey."

42  What would you do if you
were in the pastor's shoes?

Maurice Cooney in "The Challenge of the Priesthood" describes
the role of the priest today.

## 29 NO GREATER CHALLENGE

The young girl was pretty and frightened. . . . Her face
crumpled a bit as she told me, "I'm going to have a baby. I'm
not married and the boy I love has left me. I wish I were dead."
. . . "What can I do? I don't think my parents want me back.
I've thought of killing myself." I told her that God loved her and
the baby too; and that it would be a mean trick to kill herself and
the baby when God was trying so hard to save her.

Then I told her she could relax; we'd get her home and that
I was sure the parents would welcome her. When I told her that
Christ loved her, she smiled and cried at the same time . . .

Cancer and alcohol

With a few nasty thoughts about the boy who left her that way,
I walked upstairs to another ward where a good lady from the
parish had just been informed that she has cancer. I thought I
would try to cheer her up but when I walked in she said, "Hi,
Father" and smiled brilliantly. Her conversation was normal and,
as I left her, I gave her a blessing. . . . I feel better.

A man comes to the rectory door. "Father, I'm an alcoholic,
but I've been dry for six months. Right now I just have to have a
drink; help me." I bring him in, and phone the A.A.'s. No answer.
I think about some ex-alkies in the parish and phone them all--

no answer. I tell the man, "Come on, we're going for a ride."
Maybe I can find one of my ex-drunks. Thank heaven one of them
is working in his garden. I introduce them, and Frank says, "It's
okay, Father, I'll look after him, he can stay with us." A real
brotherhood--the A.A.'s.

## Red star

It's 10:00 p.m. and the phone rings. "Father, it's the Mental
Hospital. We have a man here named John S. He's been here since
1920 and the doctor has put him on Red Star." I get the oils and
hurry to the hospital on the hill. A smiling male nurse admits me
to the infirmary and I come face to face with John S.

I say to John, "I am going to give you the sacrament of the sick."
I hope somewhere in that cloudy world of John's that he can make
an act of the will to love God. John slowly takes his hand out of his
mouth and says, "Will it hurt?" I tell him no, that it won't hurt
because we don't use needles to anoint people. "Okay," he says
and replaces his hand in his mouth . . .

## Voice in the dark

I open the door of the confessional, turn on the light and, sitting
down, I open my breviary. . . . A hesitant voice breaks in from
the darkness to my right. "Father, I haven't been to confession
for years. I want to come back; help me." I listen to the recital
of the abandoned years, and thrill to the last words "O God, I am
sorry."

Christ's mercy has pursued this man and now He . . . uses the
absolution of my words to wipe out the past and I say to the man,
"Go in peace," and he does.

43 What do people look for most
in a priest? Would being married
tie a priest down too much?

## Identity crisis

This is my work; I am a priest. . . .

My task is to bring Christ and His people together; to show men
that Christ does care about them. I have to show the general man-
ager and the delivery boy that in the gentle eyes of Christ they are
of equal value.

Man in this century is told that he is expendable. They tell him that he is probably just a chance collection of atoms and that therefore he isn't worth much, and in the next breath tell him that he is a god who is destined to rebuild the earth. There isn't much evidence for either hypothesis.

The only gauge of man's value lies in the value that was put on humanity by Jesus Christ. He thought it worthwhile to suffer for us and die for us. I have to try to show that to people. There is no greater challenge than that. I am a priest; I wouldn't want it any other way.

44 Why is being a priest a big challenge today? Does it disturb you that a number of priests have left the priesthood recently?

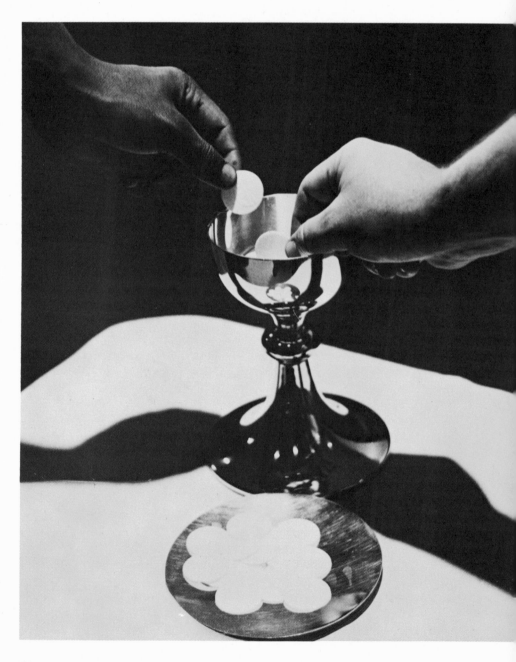

## 30 BLACK CONVERT

Phyllis Wiggins in "A New Member Speaks Out" calls for dialogue within the Church.

We seldom hear the word <u>convert</u> today. And that is good.
The Catholic who entered the Church as an adult no longer feels
that he can never quite "belong." He likes the new emphasis on
the Church as the Family of God and no longer feels that . . .
his own relatives and friends are somehow spiritually undesir-
able because they have not gone through a "conversion."

### Dialogue needed

. . . But many converts wish that dialogue would begin within
the Church. We see it as our deepest need. . . .
It is difficult for us to understand some of the criticisms our
"cradle-Catholic" brothers sometimes make of the Family. For
example, the first impression of suppression that most Negro
converts receive soon after they come into the Church, is not
from the official Church as so many modern Catholics complain.
The great wonder to us is how the laity ignore the official teachings of their Church on this matter of racial discrimination.
In his "Studies in Race Relations," Father Eugene McManus
cites the fact that since 1937, there have been some 14 papal
documents on the subject with some 20 from the bishops of the
world, including two from South Africa, to say nothing of those

which have come from the hierarchy since 1961 when Father
McManus' book was written!

45 Black militants openly accuse
the Church of being racist. How
do they get this impression?

## Reserved seats

Yet when I started down the main aisle of a midwestern Catholic
church, five weeks after my conversion, an excited usher appeared,
it seemed from nowhere.
"Young lady," he said. "You can't sit in this aisle. It's reserved."
Other parishioners were sitting in that section of the church,
though I was not unaware that the handful of Negro parishioners
always sat in the St. Joseph's transept.
"Just the psychological defense of my people who fear rebuff,"
I had always thought.
. . . The next Sunday, I was present at that same aisle and took
a seat in the third pew from the front of the church. My usher friend
apparently filled all the pews around mine and when he had no more
available seats, he filled my pew.
That was the end of segregated seating in that church . . .

46 What is meant by the
phrase "psychological defense"?

## No guts

Often, Negro converts suspect that the official teachings of
the Church have not taken root, even within the Church itself,
because laymen haven't had the intestinal fortitude to see that
Catholics practice what they preach. The hierarchy can only
make statements. We, who are an integral part of the scene,
must see that those official statements take flesh--through us!

## White man's Church?

. . . In the early days of my conversion, it was the determined
stand of Archbishop Joseph Ritter against too many of his protesting
laymen which bolstered my confidence in the social commitment
of the Church. . . . And when Rome upheld his stand it soothed
the agony I had suffered when my dad was unhappy about my be-

coming Catholic because, "The Church was the Church of the white man!"

Similar statements from black men don't always mean that they are personally acquainted with vicious prejudiced Catholics. My dad knew few Catholics on a personal basis.

His stand was that . . . [t]he majority of today's civil rights leaders were formed within the Protestant churches.

This does not mean that the Protestant religion has been a subterfuge for creating social protest, but it has been a big factor in inspiring black men with a sense of their God-given dignity. . . . [T]o accuse the Catholic Church of being a bastion of prejudice because so few Negroes have become Catholic is foolish. Like my dad, most Negroes simply face the social facts of life: "What chance is there for a Negro to develop his leadership potential, even in a Church, where he is a numerical minority?"

Social agency?

In our day of racial crisis, does the average Negro wish to see his own parish become . . . a mere social agency?

If white Catholics were aware that many Negroes in parishes which have become deeply involved in the racial situation leave that parish for others which are less involved, the answer would be obvious. In such instances it is often the new breed of white Catholic, straining for social action, who comes into the inner city parish as its stable black membership exits, leaving the parish a white island in the midst of a black ghetto.

Nor does it mean that Negroes don't wish to see the Church involved in their own social cause. It has been the inability of the "liberal" Catholic and the "conservative" to dialogue, in respect and love on race within the Church, which has made black men suspicious of the sincerity of those Catholics who have a real desire to bring social justice to us. For this reason, above all, the Negro who is Catholic must speak out, no matter how much black or white men try to silence us!

47 What is the author's point about having black parishes degenerate into social agencies? Why do blacks sometimes suspect white "liberals"?

## 31 THE SUNDAY HANG UP

I first became aware of the parish Mass problem last summer
in July. My cousin had been staying over at my house, and on
Sunday we rode our bikes to church.

On the way, he suggested that we ditch Mass. I asked him why
he wanted to do that. He replied that the Mass was boring . . .
it did not inspire him. I said that even if it is boring, we really
should go.

We didn't ditch that Mass. But the long ceremony in the hot,
stuffy church certainly did not make us any better Christians.

I think this incident illustrates what is wrong with the Church
today. It is simply not appealing to young people, and they are
turned off by the rituals. Take, for instance, the hymns that
are sung in most churches. They are usually sung without any
feeling or emotion. . . . Sometimes these tunes are childish.
Another point about hymns is that at some churches, the same
hymns are used week after week, which makes them twice as
boring.

The homilies, too, are long and boring. The priest should
either choose better topics, or shorten the homily to five or ten
minutes, instead of the twenty minutes it usually is now.

Those are the kinds of things that turn young people away from
Sunday Mass and cause them to lose their faith. Something has
to be done, but what?

48 Would you agree with what this boy says? What can be done about the situation?

Spiritual kick

Commenting on the above boy's problem, someone had this to say. I agree that in many parishes the Mass does not grab young people. Two points should be made clear.

First, somewhere along the line, young people have been given a bum steer by some teacher--or parent. Through no fault of their own, they have been given the idea that the Mass should give them some kind of a spiritual kick. All they have to do is sit there and listen, and suddenly they will be turned on.

Nothing could have been further from Christ's mind. At the Last Supper, he said, "Do this in memory of me." He did not say, "Let this be done to you in memory of me." This means we are to involve ourselves in the Mass. No one commissioned the priest to do this for us. To quote an old, but very true, cliché, "You get out of something only what you put into it." This is even more true of the Mass.

Stop eating?

The second point that should be made is this. The Mass is a meal. It is doing what Christ did at the Last Supper--which was eating a meal. The fact that Christ put the Mass in the form of a meal was no accident. For apart from being a time when we offer ourselves with Christ to the Father, the Mass is also a time when we are spiritually nourished.

Now supposing you joined the Peace Corps and are stationed on an island which is visited once every six months by boat. Suppose that after the first week on the island, you find that the food there is lousy. In fact, it makes you so sick that you sometimes throw up. Would you stop eating because the food was so lousy? If you did, you wouldn't be around to welcome the boat when it returned in six months. No matter how unappealing the food was, you realize that it's all you have. To stop eating would be to run the risk of physical starvation and death.

So, too, with the Mass. It may not appeal to you as much as you might like, but to stop eating at the Lord's table would be to risk spiritual starvation and spiritual death.

In summary, then, I am saying two things. First, many young

people have been misled. This is not their fault, but the fact remains that they were led to expect something that Christ never intended. This must now be corrected. Most young people have the ability and the good will to make this adjustment when it is pointed out to them.

Second, we need to keep working on the Mass, so that young people will find it easier to involve themselves in it as active participants. Until an effective means is developed, young people cannot afford to miss the Lord's Supper. To do so would be to invite spiritual starvation and ultimate spiritual death. Most young people, also, have the good sense and intelligence to understand this.

### Peer pressure

But having made these two points, a more serious problem arises. Even when young people appreciate and accept the two points just made, they sometimes run into a more difficult problem. It is well described by a Chicago teen-ager. He wrote:

For the past few Sundays, I have observed that teen-age participation at Mass is almost nonexistent. The Mass I regularly attend is set up specifically for teen-agers. It is set in an in-the-round arrangement with six guitarists. Still, many teen-agers (including myself) merely go through the motions, never really bothering to participate fully.

The only way I can account for this situation is that most teenagers adhere to the principle of not blowing your cool. You are regarded as flakey or corny by your friends if you really involve yourself in the Mass as much as you sometimes want to. I know for a fact that the very same people who cannot wait for the priest to say, "Go, the Mass is ended," would be the most active participants if they were on a private retreat. I, for one, would like to participate in the Mass, if it were the accepted thing to do.

I have tried different approaches to remedy this problem. First, I got up enough courage one Sunday to bring a youth hymnal to use at Mass. But my friends' wise remarks and smirking faces made me quickly stop using it. I even tried going to different Masses and to a different parish, but it all seemed rather pointless. What is the solution?

49 How does this teen's problem differ from the first boy's problem?

Mixed up

Even when a young person successfully handles the problem
of involving himself in the Mass, and even when he has the independence and maturity to withstand the peer pressure, he may
experience an even more serious problem with regard to the
Mass. The following essay by a midwestern high-school student,
describes the problem well.

I attend Mass regularly every Sunday, but I don't participate in
it. My parents say the problem is that I am lazy. This is partly
true. But right now I am mixed up about the Mass and my religion.
The attendance at Mass for most of the young people today is the
same way.
Recently, the Church declared that some forty different saints
did not live and that we don't have to respect the days that were
set aside for them. When this was said, I began to wonder if the
Church was real. At Mass I don't know if I should believe in the
Church or not.

> 50  How does this student's
> problem differ from the previ-
> ous two?

Inner conflict

The reasons why young people find difficulty with the Mass
fall into various categories. What may be a difficulty for one
young person is not necessarily a difficulty for another. Only by
isolating my problem can I hope to work out a solution to it.
Here is one teen-ager's attempt to do this.

As you sit waiting for Mass to start, the dimmed lights of the
church gradually become brighter. Over in a corner bench, a kid
dressed in khakis and a dirty sport shirt is reading a comic book.
He seems very engrossed in it, too. Through the window vents in
the wall, you hear little kids laughing and screaming; you hear
the cars and buses rumble past; from the hotel across the street,
you hear a drunken man drawl out the words, "I'll kill you, woman."
Statues of saints adorn the pulpit. On the right side is a life-
sized statue of Martin de Porres, the brown-skinned saint. His
statue is erect, his forehead has no wrinkles, his eyes are not

bloodshot, and not the slightest trace of fatigue mars his face. You might say to yourself, Why are the living saints of today so different from the saints of the past? Why do the people I look up to as being good have wrinkles of worry and bags under their eyes? Why do they, unlike the saints of the past, display the physical fatigue associated with hard work and mental stress? Incongruous? Apparently so.

Then, the nun begins to play the organ, and the priest and altar boys come out. The priest says, "I will go to the altar of God." The altar boys say, "To God who gives joy to my youth." I think this is perhaps where the essence of my problem concerning faith lies. I cannot honestly say that God gives joy to my youth. As a matter of fact, the concept of God stymies me. Maybe this is partially because he seems so unreal, so non-existent. And going to church definitely does not boost my faith or make me more religious. In regard to other people--the ones I care for in particular--I would love to dislike them just as much if I didn't go to church or belong to the Catholic faith. So why all the fuss about going to church? Perhaps--as a matter of fact, probably--I'm ignorant. I probably don't know enough about the value of religion in one's life. But at this stage, it seems I would have to take a course in theology in order to set myself straight. However, this would seem to be impractical.

Generally, I feel as though I would be doing the right thing by being more devout, yet there seems to be no logical reason for actually being this way. Irritatingly enough, I can aptly state the situation, but I still can't adequately handle it. So where does that leave me and hordes of others who have the same general attitude? Maybe nowhere; maybe closer to the truth than ever before.

51  What is the boy's point about: 1) the statue, 2) ignorance of theology, 3) being closer to the truth than ever before?

## 32 SNOWBOUND

A senior describes three Masses
that held real meaning for him.

During the Big Snow a few winters back, a busload of fifty of
us were returning to Chicago following a retreat. The snowbound
roads halted our trip, and we had to seek temporary shelter in
a school basement.

For three days we were confined. But each day we were able
to attend Mass together. It was surprising to see and to feel the
unity of the group during these Masses. The guitar music, the
singing, and the group spirit, combined to make these the most
rewarding experiences of our lives.

Why were we able to achieve such unity during these Masses?
Why can't we achieve a similar unity in every Mass? These are
the questions that now haunt us as we look back.

Lord, help us to attain unity with our fellowmen through you
in the sacrifice of the Mass.

"I pray that they may all be one. O Father . . . just as you
and I are one . . ." John 17:21-22.

52  How would you answer the
questions in the third paragraph?

## 33 CROSS-COUNTRY

A student explains why and how the
Mass became meaningful for him.

When I went out for the cross-country team, I expected it to be tough, but it has turned out to be great. When all the guys are out there warming up, you feel so good inside that you want the whole world to know it. One of the times I felt best was during a four-mile warm-up. Everyone was happy, because we just won a big meet the day before. All the guys were talking it up--how we might take State in a couple of years. (It made me proud to be a part of all this.) After we finished 3 1/2 miles, we still kept up the chatter--talking about anything and everything.

When we finished, everyone looked so exhausted, that some people might have felt sorry for us. But inside we felt so good we could cry. Inside me was a wonderful feeling. All these guys were related to me in a special way; we all shared this moment of deep ecstasy together.

Another great experience has been the weekly Mass that the team attends together. It has given me new faith, not like the old, but different; because I share the Mass with all these guys.

I love cross-country and wish it could last all year. It has helped me to discover the real meaning of Christian love; and I am a better person for this experience.

53  How can a team Mass both express and form team spirit?

## 34 NEW FAITH

You are moving from childhood
faith to a mature adult faith.

Crossing the bridge from childhood to adulthood can cause
problems in the home world. This same transition can cause
even greater problems in the parish world.

For just as you are going through a physical change, so you
are also going through a faith change. You are now moving away
from a childhood faith to an adult faith. Only by understanding this
change can you understand the problems that you now face--or
may soon face--in your parish world. The Mass problem is only
one manifestation of a wider problem: crossing over from a
childhood to an adult faith.

### Growth

In your childhood, you based your faith heavily upon the adult
world. When you were little, your belief in the Trinity rested,
for the most part, on your faith in what your parents or teachers
told you. They said there were three persons in God, and you
took their word for it. You did not quibble about it.

By the time you got to high school, you were well aware that
your parents and teachers are not infallible. This raised an important question in your mind--or should have raised it. "Do I
believe in Christ or the Trinity merely because I was told to
believe in them?"

82

So it is with the man who on his deathbed discovers Christ. "Why did I have to go through life not knowing him?" the dying man thinks. "How much happier and richer my life would have been had I known him from childhood. How different my life would have been, had I been fired by his vision and caught up by his sense of concern for life and for other people."

56 How does a young person go about assuming personal responsibility for his faith? How can knowing Christ make one's life richer and happier?

## 36 NIGHT FLIER

Man, in this mysterious world,
will always be a night flier.

There was a time when being Catholic was less complex than today. Everything you had to do or believe was spelled out neatly in
the catechism. Now things are not so simple. Life has become
more complex; and some of the old answers and simple explanations
of the faith no longer satisfy us. As a result, Catholics of all styles
and stances are beginning to emerge. While all of them agree
pretty much on the basics of the faith, many of them disagree
drastically on how these basics should be understood.

For example, some Catholics speak of hell as if it were a
place. Others think of it as a state. Still others are not sure what
it is. This much is certain. Christ, whose record for truth goes
unchallenged by even his enemies, has assured us that hell exists.
His own efforts to describe it were in terms of eternal fire.

### Fact vs. explanation

Did Christ mean real fire? Or was he merely trying to teach
a simple people to avoid hell at all costs--as they would avoid
real fire for all eternity? Again, some Catholics disagree.

Regardless of what Christ meant, we cannot get around the
fact that he affirmed the existence of hell. If we believe in Christ,
we must also take him at his word. The fact of hell is one thing;
the explanation or description of it is a completely different thing.

This much we can say, however, hell is complete and total separation from Christ who is the source of all love, goodness, and happiness.

Perhaps the best attitude to have toward hell is that of the man who said, "Don't break your head over what hell is; break your back over how to avoid it." An electrician handling an exposed high tension wire couldn't care less that many physicists disagree on what electricity is; he is mainly concerned with not touching the wire. This, too, should be the Catholic's attitude toward hell.

When you come right down to it, there are a lot of things that we humans are in the dark about. This holds true even of the things in this world. Is it so strange, then, that we should also be in the dark about the things of the next world?

> 57 Explain the expression, "The fact is one thing; the explanation of the fact is another thing."

Night flight

In his book Night Flight, a French novelist describes the bravery of night fliers in the early days of aviation. Referring to this novel, Augustine Hennessy in "Faith Is More Than a Leap in the Dark" says:

Such a novel is not just history; it is a parable. Man in a mysterious universe has been, and always will be, a night flier. He lives and dies in the dark. His environment is a mystery to him. He is even a mystery to himself. . . . He has to get used to night flying.

It is to this night-flying man that God has spoken in the Person of His Son. God's word does not take away the night. Man, even after he becomes a believer, is still flying in the night. Truths of faith are still mysterious--much more mysterious than the secrets of the universe or the baffling mystery of man himself.

So faith is still a leap in the dark. But it is much more than a leap in the dark. It is the bravery, the hope, and the realism of a parachute jumper. God's word tells us who He is and who we are. Then it invites us to plunge into the mysterious thought-life of God Himself. God's word gives just enough light to make

man willing to take the leap. Faith is man's response to this revealing God.

The believer, like a man on a parachute, is moving in an unnatural atmosphere when he is caught up in the thought-life of God. He is not naturally at home there. He is out of his environment and only the trappings of faith--suspension lines and canopy--can keep him aloft securely enough to pass through the darkness into God's "marvelous light." (1 Peter 2:9)

Faith is not a commitment to these trappings of faith-- the formulas we rattle off in a creed. For a Christian, faith is commitment to the Person of Christ. We do not live and die for a word or a formula or a proposition that sets forth a truth about God. No words or formulas or propositions can do that adequately. We cleave to a Person by faith, and for Him we live and die.

Guide

The facts of the faith, for example hell, are like a parachute. They help us to keep from plunging to sure destruction as we journey through the mysterious night of this life. The facts of the faith, no matter how vaguely understood, are necessary to help us survive on our journey. They are like expressway signs, guiding the uncertain motorist. Without them the motorist would be confused and lost. The day will come, however, when we will be able to dispense with them, as a parachutist throws off the harness and his parachute when he reaches the ground. Until that time, however, it would be foolhardy for him to strip off his harness and chute and try to make it on his own.

As Hennessy puts it, "The last thing a man on a parachute wants to claim for himself is the right to unfettered freedom. He wants to make sure he is a man in a harness. Uninhibited freedom is for him only the freedom to die." So it is with the motorist. So it is with the Christian.

58 In what sense is faith: 1) a commitment to a person rather than to a set of statements, 2) a guide in our journey through life?

## 37 HARD TO BELIEVE?

Does Christ make it difficult
for us to believe in him?

Cathy: I really don't know why Christ made it so hard for us to believe in him. I guess he must have had a pretty good reason. Maybe he wanted faith to be some kind of challenge. We need challenges to prove to ourselves and to him that we love him.

Bill: Christ doesn't make it hard for us to believe. It's naturally hard. Faith involves a kind of giving of yourself to Christ in trust. This is not easy. Nobody makes faith hard; it's just a difficult thing for any human being to do.

Dean: Christ made it hard for us for a good reason. He wants faith to be a kind of test or screening process. He could have made it easy, but there is no challenge to that. Christ wants us to prove our love for him. He wants us to earn heaven.

Al: I don't think Christ makes it hard for us to believe. Real faith is not an easy thing to come by. The right kind of doubting is the way faith develops. For only by wrestling with the truths of your faith can you begin to understand them and make them your own. It's the way you strengthen and reaffirm your faith.

59 With whom do you most
agree? Least agree?

Rian Clancy in "Mother Church
Isn't Ann Landers" describes a
common but incorrect approach
to Christianity.

Dear Ann Landers: "My husband and I have been married for
19 years. I should only count the first ten since these last nine
years shouldn't happen to a dog."

Ann Landers, the female Moses of the 20th century, receives
hundreds of letters each month. Many of them are tragic, revealing agonizing problems of adults and teen-agers. Many of
them are answered with real sympathy and practical common
sense. But many of them cannot be answered; for easy, pat,
simple answers cannot be given to life's human, complicated
situations.

As Americans we love simple solutions. And so as American
Catholics we turn to our ecclesiastical Ann Landers in our Catholic papers and magazines. People write to the all-knowing priest
hoping that he can give them easy, simple solutions to life's
problems. One magazine recently had these zingers:

. . . "Is pre-marital sex allowed if you are in love?"

"Is it sinful to cheat the federal government on income tax?"

Stopwatch Christianity

. . . As Americans we are practical--we want to know what we
have to do--then we will do it. We want exact statistics (how many

94

baptized infants every year--this is easy--but it is not quite so
simple to find out how many teen-agers and adults grow in the love
of Christ each year). We want the exact time--the law says one
hour fast--so it is one hour fast and just too bad if that last coke
was 55 minutes before Communion. Since there are Catholics who
don't have watches and indeed tell time by the sun, it is hard to
see how this law is to be so exactly kept throughout the world.
But no matter--practical Catholicism is in our blood.

We take law literally--apply it to time zones, apply it to morals.
And so the stopwatch and the tape measure are produced to lay
down rules regarding kissing, necking, clothing, dancing. Many
Catholics love this approach to practical Catholic living--it gives
them a security; they know where they stand; there are no doubts,
problems, fears, hesitancies. All is black and white--right and
wrong. There is no middle area, for the Church has all the answers.
Ask a priest. Recently a 17-year-old at a CCD class did just that.
And the priest--not being the fourth person of the Blessed Trinity
or God Junior--didn't know and he said so. At that the fellow
launched into a diatribe, saying that the Church was failing him,
that the Church should have all the answers.

> 60 How would you answer the
> boy in the CCD class? Are many
> Catholics stopwatch Christians?
> What's wrong with this approach?

A student asks a priest, "Is it
okay for me to read this book?"

Before the jet age arrived, the world was
a simple place to live in. Issues were much
more clear-cut than they are today. Take a
look at the TV Westerns. One explanation of
their popularity is that they remind us of the
good old days when life was not so complex.
Right was right, and wrong was wrong. The
good guys all wore white hats, and the bad ones
all wore black hats. The job of the Church in
such a world was quite simple. It was easy
and natural to say, "Do this! Don't do that!"

Today the world has become a far more
complicated place to live in. Let us take just
one example. Once everyone agreed that war
was morally permissible under certain circumstances. Now, however, with bombs that can
wipe out entire cities, the morality of war is
being sharply questioned. Certainly a country
has a right to defend itself against unjust attack.

But may we risk allowing two countries to
set off a nuclear nightmare in the process?
This is just one example showing how the pat
answers of the past are no longer valid today.

The Church realizes this situation and has ceased trying to play answer man to every issue. Instead she concentrates on trying to explain to modern man what Christ said about life, its purpose, and how man should strive to live it. It is up to individuals and to nations to apply Christ's words to daily life. This is why God gave them an intellect, a free will, and a conscience.

The Church was founded by Christ to preach God's word and to assist mankind to live it. On some basic questions the Church still can and must speak out as to how Christ's word applies to this or that area of life. In most cases, however, she cannot and should not. The reason: the issues are far too complex and complicated. In such cases her duty is to remind experts and governments of their grave responsibility to sift all the facts, and then, in the light of Christ's message, to follow the proper course of action.

## Is it wrong?

A student asks a priest, "Is it wrong for me to read this book?" To answer this question accurately the priest would have to know the boy and the book thoroughly. Oftentimes he doesn't know either that well. Obviously, the priest cannot--and should not-- say yes or no to the student's question. Rather, he should help the student to answer the question for himself.

For example, the priest should ask the student why he wants to read the book. Is it merely out of curiosity because of what others have said about it? Or is it because the book was assigned by his college professor?

Next, the priest should ask why the student thinks that the book might possibly be wrong for him to read. Is it because he fears it might shake his faith deeply? Or is it because the book might cause him other problems?

In the light of these questions, the student can then decide whether his reasons for wanting to read the book justify the risk he takes in reading the book.

61 What would be some weighty reasons for reading a dangerous book? Would some books require weightier reasons than others? Explain.

## Cases vary

It should be noted here that one student might read a certain book with profit and without experiencing any serious problems, while another student might read the same book and experience severe problems. Oddly enough, therefore, a priest who knew two students very well, might urge one student to read a certain book and advise another not to read it.

Because human nature is what it is, however, one can safely predict that certain books, as a rule, will cause serious problems for the average person. The same goes for certain kinds of movies. For the average person to ignore completely the guidance of experienced experts in these matters would be foolhardy. It would be like a patient who ignored a doctor's warning not to take a certain pill.

It is entirely possible that you are exceptional, and not average, but you would have to have good evidence that this is the case, before acting contrary to expert advice.

> 62 What is meant by the expression, "human nature being what it is"? What is meant by "average person" as it is used above?

## No contradiction

One final point, how can two different priests give opposite answers to the same question? This can happen when the question asked is one that admits of a personal or theological opinion. Take the case of war again. One priest may believe in conscience that modern war is justified under certain circumstances. Another might believe in conscience that modern war is never justified under any circumstances. Their advice to a young man who inquired about the morality of active combat service might, therefore, be completely different. Actually, both priests would be better off to give the facts as they see them, and then tell the young man to decide for himself. Of course, if the young man found it impossible to make up his mind and still sought advice, the picture is changed. He will naturally get two different views from two different priests.

> 63 Has this essay cleared up any questions which you have had in this area? Explain.

## 40 THE PARATROOPERS

Sarah Boyden in "An Awakening Interest in the ESP Mystery" describes a minister's experience.

"Three rather beat-up looking young men were waiting to see me when I got back to my visitor's quarters at Fort Bragg, N.C., about 11:30 one evening recently," said the Rev. Arthur Ford, a minister widely known for his mediumistic powers.

"Some of the chaplains at the fort had invited me to come there and talk to the paratroopers about psychic proofs of life after death. Believe me, these men, about to take off for duty in Viet Nam, were mighty interested in the subject. They kept me talking for 2 1/2 hours after it was over. But those three men insisted on seeing me then and there. Maybe I would believe them, they said. No one else would.

"They were survivors of a group of 10 paratroopers who, through an error, landed among the enemy line instead of behind their lines. Seven were instantly killed. The three, desperately wounded, were left for dead by the enemy.

"'None of us alive could move,' they said. 'Our walkie-talkies were wrecked, but none of us could speak, anyway. We were all conscious, though. Suddenly we saw one of our dead pals get up and walk over and stand beside us--it was very strange, as he looked just like always, except his body also seemed to be lying on the ground behind him while he stood there. We didn't hear him say anything, but he smiled, and we each got the feeling that everything would be all right.

"'Ten minutes later, a rescue helicopter picked us up. We asked the pilot how he knew we were there.' 'I didn't,' he said. 'I was going back to base, nowhere near here, when I suddenly felt as if a commanding officer spoke, directing me to this spot. Something actually made me come down here--it seemed to be a person but I couldn't see him. I was really brought, no doubt about that.'"

Ford said he believed them and called it "one more indication that man personally survives physical death."

64 List the pros and cons for accepting this as "one more indication that man personally survives physical death."

## Life after death

Opinions may vary whether the paratrooper incident is an indication that man personally survives after death. It is strange, however, that at the moment when some people are beginning to question life after death, psychiatric researchers and Nobel prize-winning scientists are beginning to talk about it with greater seriousness and frequency.

The term we give to survival after death is immortality. Commenting on immortality, Dr. Hornell Hart, professor emeritus of sociology of Duke University says, "My belief in immortality has been immeasurably strengthened by psychiatric research."

He went on to say that over "three million tests, such as those carried out at Duke . . . have demonstrated that the human mind can function independently of space and time as we understand them."

## Face in the night

In her exciting book, A Search for Truth, Ruth Montgomery describes an incident that seems to demonstrate the mind's ability to "function independently of space and time as we understand them."

One rainy January night, the wife of General Nathan F. Twining, commander of the 13th Air Force, was awakened in her North Carolina home by a sound like a thunderclap. Leaping up, she saw her husband standing at the foot of her bed--although she knew at this very minute he was on active duty in the Pacific.

"I saw Nate's face and hands clearly, even his West Point ring. As I watched, his fingers lost their grip on the footboard of the

102

bed and gradually disappeared."

She said the experience was so vivid and strange that "the hair literally stood up" on the nape of her neck.

Exactly three days later, she received word from the Air Force that her husband was missing. His plane had crashed at sea the night of her vision. Six days after the vision, the general was spotted on a life raft and rescued from the stormy seas. He knew nothing of his wife's hair-raising experience. But in his first letter back to her, he described a strange experience he had as his plane was crashing into the sea. He saw her face vividly and clearly, peering at him through the rain.

Was the whole episode a mere coincidence? Or was there something deeper involved? These are questions that still haunt both husband and wife.

65 How would you be inclined to answer the above questions?

Beyond the senses?

Extrasensory perception, popularly known as ESP, means that we sometimes know or experience something without the known use of our five senses: seeing, hearing, smelling, touching, or tasting.

Related to ESP is mental telepathy. That is we sometimes seem to be able to communicate with another person without speech, words, or signals.

Related to ESP is, also, clairvoyance. That is we sometimes seem to know that some event has happened, even though we have received no direct knowledge about it.

Many experiments have been performed to prove or disprove extrasensory perception. One of the more famous centers of experimentation has been Duke University. Though striking facts have been turned up, experts still debate the subject. Experimentation is still in a pioneer stage of development. Some preliminary conclusions seem to be the following: 1) that ESP takes place, 2) that all people possess it to some extent, and 3) that ESP often takes place unconsciously and unintentionally.

66 Have you ever experienced ESP in any way? Why does Dr. Hart feel that ESP supports the idea of immortality?

## 41 GREEN SLIVER

> Death is not the end of life; it
> is the transformation of life.

Psychiatric researchers are not the only ones who endorse the belief of man's survival after death. Dr. Arthur Compton, the Nobel prize-winning physicist, thinks that the nobility of man requires such a survival. He says, "It takes a lifetime to build the character of a noble man. . . . Having been thus perfected, what shall nature do with him? Annihilate him? What infinite waste! I . . . believe he lives after death."

Dr. Wernher von Braun, the top United States rocket and space expert, says, "Science . . . tells us that nothing in nature . . . can disappear without a trace. Nature does not know extinction. All it knows is transformation." He concludes by saying that science "strengthens my belief in the continuity of our spiritual existence after death."

### Christ

What psychiatric research (three million tests) hints at, and what science points at, was preached by Jesus Christ with unmistakable clarity: "Man survives after death." This fact is at the heart and center of Christ's teaching. Constantly, he spoke of eternal life, and the kingdom of God. No message in the Gospel comes home more forcefully than this one.

What are some of the things Christ says about life after death?

104

First of all, Christ makes it clear that life after death should not be conceived as something completely cut off from our present life. Christ clearly taught that life after death is not a new life that we will suddenly begin to possess. On the contrary, it will be a continuation of our present life. Rather, death is the gateway or passage to eternal life. This idea is beautifully brought out by the following note which was found in the wallet of Colonel Marcus of the Israeli army when he was killed in battle.

> I am standing upon the seashore. A ship at my side spreads her white sails to the morning breeze and starts for the blue ocean. She is an object of beauty and strength, and I stand and watch her until at length she is only a ribbon white cloud just where the sea and sky come to mingle with each other. Then someone at my side says, "There! She's gone!"
>
> Gone where? Gone from my sight--that is all. She is just as large in mast and hull and spar as she was when she left my side, and just as able to bear her load of living freight-- to the place of destination. Her diminished size is in me, not in her, and just at the moment when someone at my side says, "There! She's gone!" there are other voices ready to take up the glad shout, "There! She comes!" And that is dying.

Colonel Marcus' description of death is both accurate and excellent. For death is, above all, a passage--a passage from this life to life everlasting.

## Transformation

Second, Christ taught that death is not only a continuation of this life, but a transformation of it. You might compare our present life to a seed from which eternal life will someday sprout forth. The seed (this life) must die before the new life (life eternal) can emerge from it. An example will help.

Shortly after President Kennedy's death, a little boy came running up to his kindergarten teacher and said, "He's dead. I tell you he's dead. I saw the fire on top of the dirt. He's dead."

The teacher paused a moment and thought. She wanted to explain to the little boy that President Kennedy was not dead in the sense that she was afraid the little boy thought him to be.

After a moment's reflection, she took the child over to the window box, where she and the children had planted a seed about a week before. Taking her finger, she scraped beneath the dirt to

where the seed was planted. It was now beginning to sprout.
Pointing to the tiny green sliver, the teacher said, "See the seed.
Something is happening to it. It is decaying, but at the same time,
something new is also happening--something wonderful and beautiful. The seed is changing its way of living. It is passing over from
being a seed to that for which the seed was made--to be a plant.
That is what is happening to President Kennedy. He is passing
over from the imperfect life which he had to the more perfect life
for which he was made."

Death is not the end of life. Rather it is the continuation of
life in a more full and more perfect way. Death is the transformation of our present life into that for which we were made.

Death is a constant reminder to us that this life is merely
the prelude to life eternal.

67 What point about death is il-
lustrated by the: 1) ship story,
2) Kennedy story?

## 42 THE SKID

*Someone swore; the rest of us*
*were dazed and silent.*

While speeding down a freeway one rainy evening, my car skidded out of the right-hand lane, swerved, and missed a lamp-post by inches. My friends and I got out of the car. Someone swore; the rest of us were dazed and silent. We got back into the car and continued on. The incident got no news--made no headlines. The unspoken question in each boy's mind was, "How prepared was I to die?"

The incident reminded me that I will have to die one day, possibly unexpectedly. It gave me a chance to reflect upon the pattern of my life.

Help me to realize, Lord, that this life was meant to be a prelude and preparation for life after death.

"What does it profit a man to gain the whole world and to suffer the loss of his own soul." Matthew 16:26.

68 What was the closest brush you ever had with death? Would you prefer to die quickly and unexpectedly or slowly and knowingly? Why?

A split second before I went out,
something amazing happened.

## 43 UNFORGETTABLE

Eternal life means sharing Christ's risen life. Eternal life is
not something that will begin after death. We already share Christ's
risen life--in seed form.

A Christian does not believe in future life; he believes in eternal life. But if it is eternal, then it has already begun. We are
now living it--in an imperfect way. Death does not end life; it
transforms it. After death we will possess and share Christ's
risen life in a fuller more perfect way.

Sharing Christ's risen life means that we die to selfishness
and self-centeredness and take up a new life of maturity and
personal concern for other people. It means living the life which
Christ gave us in baptism and continues to deepen in us through
our faith-encounters with him in the sacraments.

Shot of morphine

Recently, a priest at Loyola University in Chicago was sitting
in his office. There was a knock at the door. "Come in," he said.
With that a former student opened the door and hobbled in on
crutches. He had just returned from Vietnam, where he had lost
a leg from misdirected American mortar fire.

In the conversation that followed, the young man described the
events following the unfortunate accident.

First, he recalled lying on the ground covered with blood and wanting to stay conscious so that he could pray. Second, he recalled being hoisted aloft into a helicopter. Third, he recalled being stretched out on a table with lights glaring down on him. Then, he recalled a face appearing very close to his saying, "Are you sorry for your sins?" "Hell yes, I'm sorry," he shot back.

With that the young man felt a hand touch his forehead. A priest was giving him the sacrament of the Anointing of the Sick. Immediately something remarkable happened. The young man described it.

> Then a split second before I went out, I felt oil on my forehead, and something happened which I'll never forget; something which I have never experienced before in my life! All of a sudden I stopped gasping for every inch of life; I just burst with joy and thought I'm ready to die, please take me, I'm ready. I knew at worst I'd spend a while in purgatory but I felt like I just got a shot of a million CC's of morphine. I was on cloud No. 9; I felt free of body and mind.
>
> After this about three or four times I was conscious during a ten-day period and never worried about dying; in fact, I was waiting for it.

## Real contact

When we were young, we may have thought of the sacraments as things to be done to get grace. We may even have looked upon them as recharging stations where we recharged our spiritual batteries. This childhood notion of the sacraments is a far cry from what is really the case.

The sacraments are, first and foremost, living encounters with Christ. Through the sacraments we come into real live contact with Christ.

## Personal

When Christ was on earth in human form, he acted in men's lives in a concrete way. With the touch of his suntanned hand, he healed the sick. With the words of his strong voice, he forgave men, taught people, and prayed to his Father.

Today, Christ still acts in men's lives in a concrete, personal way. He does this, especially through the Mass and the sacraments. We may make this comparison. Just as Christ acted in a concrete

way in gospel times by the personal actions of his human body,
so Christ acts in a concrete way today by the liturgical actions
of his mystical body.

69 How does the Loyola student's
experience point up the fact that
the sacraments are personal
encounters with Christ? Explain:
liturgical action, mystical body.

## Time of crisis

The Loyola student's experience is also an excellent illustration
of how Christ acts in our lives through the sacrament of the Anointing of the Sick. How so? Let us approach it this way.

Have you ever tried to study when you had a splitting headache?
Have you ever tried to pray when tortured by a severe toothache?
These examples show how even minor bodily ailments impair
spiritual or intellectual activity. Bodily pain can so depress us
spiritually that we don't care what happens. Bodily pain has even
driven people to suicide. The Christian sacrament of the Anointing of the Sick must be seen in this context.

Jesus Christ knew the power of pain to weaken the spirit. He
felt its crushing effect himself. It was for this reason, among
others, that he worked so many healing miracles for the people
of his time. It is also for this reason, among others, that he in-
structed his priests to "anoint the sick." James 5:14-15.

## Strength and forgiveness

Christ wanted to strengthen and to comfort us in times of serious sickness or accident. Christians believe that Jesus Christ gave
his Church the sacrament of the Anointing of the Sick to give them
special help in times of special crises. Christians believe that
when the sacrament is given by a priest, Christ, himself, acts
personally to strengthen and to forgive the sins of a sick person.
He is present just as certainly as when he healed and forgave
the sick in biblical times.

Experience has shown (as in the case of the young man mentioned above) that very often after receiving this sacrament, the
sick person actually experiences a physical revival of strength
and a spiritual influx of peace and calm.

Should a person die after receiving the sacrament, Christians believe that, depending on the disposition of the sick person, the effects of the sacrament can range all the way from forgiving serious sin to preparing the person for immediate union with Christ.

70 In your own words describe the purpose and the effects of Christ's action in the sacrament of the Anointing of the Sick.

> More things are wrought by pray-
> er than this world dreams of.

Eternal life is already begun within us. We possess it in seed
form. Christ planted the seed within us at baptism. But like
any seed, it must be nourished and cultivated if it is to grow into
what it was intended to be.

The chief means of nourishing and cultivating the seed of eternal life is the sacraments. We can no more expect to grow to
spiritual maturity without the sacraments than we can expect to
grow to physical maturity without eating.

Besides the sacraments, another key aid to growing to spiritual
maturity is prayer.

## Surprising

Many young people have a natural prayer instinct. Yet, through
no fault of their own, many of them are surprisingly ignorant about
prayer. Worse yet, many of them think that prayer is merely asking for things: to find a lost wallet, to pass a history exam, to win
an important basketball game. This attitude is unfortunate, because it reduces God merely to the role of a need-filler.

As we saw last year, prayer normally takes three forms: meditation, contemplation, or direct address. Often these three forms
occur woven together in one and the same prayer--just as three
strands of cord are woven together in one and the same rope.

Meditation is a kind of thinking about God or the problems of my life in a deep way. Meditation can be planned. That is, I can deliberately set out to meditate. For example, I can walk out across a golf course after dark with the specific intention of thinking out some problem.

On the other hand, meditation can drift in upon me unexpectedly. To illustrate how this can work, here is an actual experience written by a high-school student.

One day after playing a hard basketball game, I went to a fountain nearby for some water. The cool water tasted good, and I felt refreshment come into my tired, sore body. I depended on water for refreshment and strength. Where does water come from? Clouds. Where are clouds from? Vaporized air. This went on until I got no answer. Or rather, I was left with only one answer. God! For the next couple of minutes, I just sat there kind of overpowered by what God must be like.

## Spellbound

Meditation usually leads to contemplation or direct address. Contemplation is a kind of mental gazing at God. During such a prayer, I am so caught up with the idea of God that I can hardly utter a single word. It is like listening to a great piece of music, or gazing spellbound at a stunning view of nature. The example described by the high-school boy is an illustration of how meditation can end in contemplation. Observe how the boy said, "For the next couple of minutes, I just sat there kind of overpowered by what God must be like."

## Innermost feelings

Meditation can also end in direct address. Unlike contemplation, which is a kind of silent basking in some big idea, and unlike meditation which is a kind of mental dialogue with myself or God, direct address is a statement of my innermost feelings to God. I express my sorrow for having been disloyal to him, I ask his help, I thank him, or just share my thoughts with him. Here is an example written by a high-school boy.

Lord, today I feel like quitting, but yet I don't want to. It is a strange feeling--wanting to do something and then not wanting to do it. I seem to have lost all confidence in myself. It seems like everyone else is confident in himself, but somehow I'm not. I wish somebody would tell me what is going on. I'm just not with it. Help me, Lord.

## Ping-pong paddle

Sometimes meditation, contemplation, and direct address weave themselves tightly together so that it is hard to tell when one begins and the other ends. The following is a good example of this.

When I was a boy, there were many times when I prayed out of fear. Such was the case when I would lose some money, or my jacket, or a credit card. I can remember running feverishly back along the route I had taken before, searching everywhere for the lost item. At these times I was inclined to pray madly, asking God to help me find what I lost. At the same time, I promised never to commit a sin again. But these instances were so commonplace (as you might guess) that I would not consider them as real prayer, but more of a reflex action on my part.

I think the first time that I really prayed was about five years ago when I attended my first wake. As my sister and I knelt down in front of the body, I was shocked to see the makeup that covered, what I realized for the first time, was a lifeless shell. This person, my father's uncle, whom I had known well, was really dead. And what I saw before me was nothing more than a nothing, a giant hoax.

As I looked at the corpse, all I could think about was the funny way he used to hold a ping-pong paddle. I couldn't get this picture out of my mind. Oddly enough, this is what drove me to real prayer. I prayed with all my soul, both for my uncle and for myself. Perhaps (I now realize) because I was once at the other end of a ping-pong table with a man who now needed makeup to keep his face from falling apart.

71 Why do you think meditation usually ends in contemplation or direct address? When was the last time you really prayed? Explain.

> The fact that we did it once
> means that we can do it again.

## 45  ABILITY AND STYLE

Many young people have experienced moments of real prayer
in their lives. We might compare these exceptional experiences
to what occasionally happens to an amateur at sports. A very poor
golfer will sometimes get off a great shot. A lousy basketball player
will sometimes sink a fantastic basket from thirty feet out. A poor
baseball player will sometimes connect with a pitch and drive it a
country mile. So it is with us in prayer. The fact that we did it
once means we can do it.

But, like the amateur athlete who must work and practice to acquire consistent ability and style, we, too, must work at prayer.
And though skill at sports is not within the reach of all of us, skill
at prayer is.

The most important step in learning to pray is learning to prepare for prayer. This is not surprising. No one with an important
job to do will approach it without careful preparation. The same
holds true for prayer.

Two approaches

When it comes to prayer, we must either seize the mood or
set the mood. Seizing the mood means that we take advantage of
those situations that sometimes come upon us spontaneously. Recall how the boy at the water fountain did not rush off. Rather he

sat down and allowed his thoughts to focus on the idea of God.

Modern man likes to think that he is in control of himself, that he is the complete master of all situations. In reality, he is often a restless being, almost incapable of standing still or concentrating. Yet this restless man wants to pray. But can he?

The answer to this question depends upon his personal willingness to step out of his whirlpool of restlessness and to compose himself. To prepare yourself for prayer means to control yourself. It means to overcome the tendency to jump up and to do what suddenly pops into your mind.

## Setting the mood

Setting the mood means that you deliberately set out to pray. This is not easy. Here's how one high-school senior attempted to set the mood. It also illustrates the self-control and effort it takes.

> I made my deepest inroad into prayer during the Milford retreat. Late at night I walked out onto the golf course and lay down on a grassy knoll. At first, I tried to think my prayers out to myself and God. It didn't work. Even though I was alone and in the mood, I could not concentrate. I didn't have the mental control to turn my thoughts to God clearly and directly. Puzzled and near frustration, I began to speak aloud. This worked, why I don't know. I found that when I talked to God, I was communicating. I needed this concrete means of communication, though. I continued a prayer to God, which I have not forgotten, and which has had fairly favorable effects on my life thus far.

## Caution

Obviously, there is small value to the mere hasty mumbling of words. Words are meaningful only if they express what we feel and think. If our prayers are merely spoken words without internal meaning, they are nothing. They are like a neatly wrapped package with no gift in it.

Nor is prayer a kind of trade with God: if you give me this, I will give you that. This kind of prayer is unworthy both of the one praying and of God. It is basically selfish. It is not the language of love and friendship. It is the language of business. Prayer comes more from the heart than from the head.

118

## Not an escape

Nor is prayer an escape from responsible action. God never intended prayer to substitute for action or for hard work. He never gave me the option of either studying to pass a test or praying to pass it. Prayer was never intended to substitute for hard work; it was meant to complement it.

A question arises. What then are we doing when we pray for help in an exam?

Among other things, we are asking God to help us to be alert. We are asking him to give us a clear mind so that we can recall what we have studied. We are asking him to keep us calm and to help us to see connections that we might normally miss. We are not necessarily asking for some minor miracle. We are normally asking God to strengthen and support our human efforts.

Something similar takes place when we pray for victory in a basketball game or a debate tournament. We are not asking God to take sides. We are merely asking him to make us alert and to capitalize on every opportunity and break. In short, we are asking God to help us to be at our very best.

Perhaps the best way to express this concretely is by the words of St. Ignatius, who said, "Act as if everything depended upon you, but pray as if everything depended upon God." This is the perfect combination. It reflects the true teamwork that should exist between prayer and action.

## The key

Anyone who values his friendship with Christ soon realizes the importance of prayer. Just as two people can never hope to develop a friendship without talking to each other frequently, so it is with Christ and you. Frequent contact is the key to friendship.

Without prayer, our friendship with Christ grows cold. You can not remain a Christian without praying any more than you can remain alive without breathing. Man needs prayer to keep alive and to grow spiritually.

Just as prayer can only spring from faith, so faith can only grow through prayer. Prayer, therefore, is not an activity that you can take or leave without faith being affected. Prayer and faith go hand in hand, just as do breath and life.

72 In your own words explain the connection between prayer and: 1) work, 2) friendship, 3) faith.

## 46 I FELL ASLEEP

> This morning I awoke, proud
> . . . but ashamed that I had failed.

Last night I lay on my bed trying to make an examination of conscience. I hardly got started when I fell off to sleep. This morning I awoke, proud that I had made an attempt at prayer, but ashamed that I had failed again to complete it.

All too often my friends and I tend to ignore the importance of prayer. Too often we don't have the courage to persevere at it. Too often we wonder if it does any good. We forget what our Lord said about prayer and how important he said it is.

Lord, help me to realize how necessary prayer is. Help me realize that it does not come easy and that I must work at it.

"Very early the next morning, long before daylight, Jesus got up and left the house. He went out of town to a lonely place where he prayed." Mark 1:35.

"Lord, teach us to pray . . ." Luke 11:1.

73 When and where do you pray best? What points does Christ make regarding prayer in Luke 11:1-13?

How do you get people to open their
minds and hearts to new ideas?

A third aid to growth in faith is the Scriptures. For the majority of Christians, the only time when they come into contact with
the Scriptures is at Mass. Without this opportunity, many Christians would lose contact with God's word completely.

In listening to the Scriptures at Mass, it is important to keep
in mind something that we said last year.

There is a big difference between hearing someone and listening to someone. Hearing is passive; listening is active. Hearing
means that I am conscious that someone is speaking, but I do not
concentrate on what he is saying. For example, while I am scanning
Time magazine, or poring over some math problem, I am aware
that someone is speaking over TV, but I do not pay attention to
what the voice is saying. I hear it, but I do not listen to it.

Active listening, on the other hand, means that I pinpoint all my
attention upon what is being said. I try to catch the words and ideas
being communicated by the speaker.

No sudden light

To listen to Christ's words with faith during the readings at Mass,
means that I do three things in particular.

First, I listen closely to the words and ideas that are being read
and explained to me.

Second, I realize that the words I hear are those of Christ, even though they come to me indirectly through Scripture and Christ's representative, the priest. The Council said, ". . . it is he [Christ] himself who speaks when the holy scriptures are read in the Church." Moreover, Christ himself told his disciples, ". . . who listens to you listens to me . . ." Luke 10:16.

Third, I believe that the Holy Spirit, whom Christ sent, is present helping me to understand Christ's words and to see how they apply to my personal life. This does not mean that I can expect to get a sudden light each time that I listen to the words of Christ at Mass. It simply means that if I do my best to listen with faith to Christ's words, the Holy Spirit will be present, in a special way, to support my human efforts.

With these points in mind, let us explore a literary form that often occurs in the Scriptures. It is the parable.

## Disbelief

When Columbus discovered America, some map makers refused for twenty years to put the new continent on their maps.

Up until the late 1960's, the members of the Flat Earth Society refused to admit the earth was round. Even when the first televised shots of the earth were relayed from outer space, some remained skeptical.

Ruth Cranston reports that when she was in China, she showed photographs of the New York skyline to the peasant Chinese. But they still refused to believe it existed. It was beyond their experience.

Skepticism is a part of our human nature. When someone tries to teach us something that goes contrary to our experience, he can expect trouble. He may even be ridiculed and looked upon as an oddball.

## Talking fish

Recently Heather Buckley used a modern parable in a magazine story. She used it to illustrate the difficulty that backers of the UFO theory have in trying to get people to even consider the possibility of UFO's.

Buckley imagined the situation of talking fish in the depths of the ocean. One day one of the fish wanders far from fish land, and stumbles upon submarines, divers, and underwater cameras invading the sea world. Excited and alarmed, the dumbfounded fish

returns to the fish village to spread the news to the local citizens
about these strange invaders from outer-water world. The poor
fish is ridiculed and made to look stupid by the local experts.
"But there can't be intelligent life up there! Too much oxygen,
not enough water, and the light would kill them. They're probably
refractions from our own system."

74 What mistake did the experts
make in their criticism? How
do we tend to make the same mistake when it comes to faith?

## Breakthrough

Thanks to this clever parable, many readers began to understand for the first time the problem the UFO theorists face. How
do you get people to widen their horizons? How do you get them to
open their minds to other possibilities of life beyond the one they
know and experience? Buckley's parable was able to open a few
minds. Why?

Readers could relate to it. They could appreciate the problem
facing the dumbfounded fish because they themselves belong to
the outer-water world. Moreover, they know that divers and submarines are actually invading the secret depths of the sea world.

The fish parable makes you stop and think. It makes you reconsider the possibility of other worlds and other forms of life
that may be totally different from our own. It does not force you
to believe that UFO's are for real, or that there is another world
of life somewhere in outer space. It only makes you reconsider
your reasons for laughing at the idea.

## More fantastic

Now supposing you went through a fantastic reincarnation. You,
a human being, were suddenly transformed into a fish--or reborn
as a fish. Supposing you wanted to tell the fish world, of which
you were now a part, about the man world to which you also belonged.

You can imagine your problem: trying to explain to them how
life lives outside of water, how people walk instead of swim,
how people fly through something called air in things called
planes, how they transport themselves on something called
wheels across something called land.

Your problem would be fantastic--almost impossible. It would not merely be a problem of trying to explain this new way of living. There would be the even greater problem of trying to get the fish people to listen to you and to take you seriously--to believe you.

75 How would you go about getting the people to listen to you and to take you seriously?

## Christ's problem

This exercise of fantasy helps you to understand the problem that confronted Christ 2000 years ago. Jesus Christ faced precisely this kind of problem. He had to get the people to listen to him and to take him seriously. Once the people began to listen to him, however, Jesus was then faced with the more difficult problem of trying to explain to the people a whole new kind of life--one that was completely foreign to their thinking. How could he possibly do this? The technique he used was the parable.

Like Buckley's parable, the parables of Christ related what the people already knew to what they didn't know. Christ's parables did not force anyone to believe any more than did Buckley's fish parable. But they did make sense. They narrowed the credibility gap. They opened people's minds and widened their horizons. People began to listen, to think, and to ask questions.

76 What did Christ do to get people to listen to him and to take him seriously?

## Our problem

Today we have become so accustomed to the gospel parables that we take them for granted, as we do air and water. We forget that Christ's parables are mind-boggling revelations of a whole new world. Through his parables, Christ puts us in touch with the world of God, an amazing world beyond human imagination.

Our problem today is to realize that when we listen to Christ's parables, we are listening to one of the most remarkable revelations ever uttered to mankind. Nothing has ever equaled them; nothing ever will. We are being put in contact with the world that "eye has not seen"--a world that is nonetheless as real to us as our own.

Christ's parables do not force us to believe. This is one of the remarkable features of a parable. They merely invite belief; they do not force it. Everyone must decide for himself whether to accept Christ and what he said. But if we accept Christ, we automatically accept what he says. He alone has seen the Father.

To accept Christ but not to accept what he said is like saying to him, "I believe in you, but not in what you say."

Christ backed up what he said by the example of his life and by his miracles. He said, "If you don't believe in me because of what I say, then believe in me because of what I do." Eventually every man must decide for himself whether to accept or to reject Christ.

> 77 In what sense is our faith placed first of all in the person, and only secondly in what he says?

Christ's parables give us insight into the world of faith.

The novel, The Heart Is a Lonely Hunter, centers around Mr.
Singer, a man who is deaf and dumb. Fortunately, Mr. Singer
can read lips. So by reading lips and writing notes, he can communicate with people.

In one episode in the novel, a teen-age girl is listening to a
record. As she listens, she tries to explain to Mr. Singer what
music sounds like. To do this, she stands in front of him, so that
he can read her lips. She also makes various gestures with her
hands and body to try to get her ideas across. After a while, she
smiles sadly and gives up. She realizes that trying to describe
sound to a deaf person is like trying to describe color to a blind
man.

The girl's difficulty was twofold. First, she found it hard to
find a sign to describe to Mr. Singer the sounds she hears. Second, even when she found a sign, she realized what a poor substitute it was for the actual sound.

78 How did Christ experience
the same twofold difficulty in
trying to teach the men of this
world about the next world?
How did parables help to bridge
the gap?

Sharper focus

The table below shows how Christ used parables to try to relate what people knew about this world to what they should know about the world of faith. It will be helpful to reread each of the three seed parables as you study the table.

| parable | gist of story | comparison | meaning |
|---|---|---|---|
| Sower Mt 13:1 | seed's fruitfulness depends on soil | planting seed like preaching God's word | fruitfulness of God's word depends on us |
| Mustard Seed Mt 13:31 | from small seed comes great tree | seed's growth like growth of kingdom | God's kingdom will start small but grow great |
| Wheat & Weeds Mt 13:24 | wheat & weeds separated at harvesttime | wheat & weeds like good & bad | good & bad separated on last day |

79 How do these three seed parables fit together into a unified whole? Why did Christ use the image of a seed? What image might he use today?

Multiple meaning

Sometimes the parables of Jesus admit of multiple (allegorical) meanings. A case in point is the Parable of the Sower, which we read above. Here is a breakdown of it.

| | |
|---|---|
| wayside | ignorant Christians |
| stony ground | fair-weather Christians |
| thorns | worldly Christians |
| good soil | loyal Christians |

Another case

Another parable that admits of multiple meanings is the Parable
of the Vinedressers in Matthew 21:33-46. Here is a breakdown of
that parable.

| parable persons | biblical persons |
|---|---|
| owner and planter | God |
| vineyard | people of Israel |
| vinedressers | Pharisees and leaders |
| servants | prophets |
| owner's son | Christ |
| new vinedressers | apostles and successors |

80 To whom did Christ address
this parable? How did they re-
act to it?

Key parables

The following table lists some key parables found in the Gospel. They deal with: 1) the nature of God's kingdom, 2) membership in it, and 3) life in it.

| nature | membership | life (duties) |
|---|---|---|
| Wedding Feast<br>Mt 22:1 | Banquet Invitation<br>Luke 14:16 | Good Samaritan<br>Luke 10:30 |
| Mustard Seed<br>Mt 13:31 | Rare Pearl<br>Mt 13:45 | Pharisee & Publican<br>Luke 18:9 |
| Vineyard Laborers<br>Mt 20:1 | Wheat & Weeds<br>Mt 13:24 | Gold Pieces<br>Luke 19:11 |

81 Choose any three parables
from the above table and show
how they apply to us today.

*Christ's parables provide us with insights into ourselves.*

## 49  RADAR SCREENS

The parables of Christ are radar screens that allow us to glimpse vaguely the contours and outlines of the world of faith. They do not begin to answer all the questions about this mysterious world. But they do give us enough information so that we can navigate through the uncertainties of this world and splash down on target in the next.

But besides acting as radar screens for the next world, parables also act as radar screens for this world. They provide us with valuable data about ourselves and how well we are navigating toward the splash-down area.

### Four friends

Recently four young people, two boys and two girls, made a high-school retreat. All of them hoped to benefit greatly from the experience. They participated in all that went on. They all made it a point to talk privately to one of the members of the retreat team who gave the retreat. Following the retreat they all discussed their experience with their school counselors.

Elaine told her counselor that she didn't get too much out of the retreat. She said it just didn't seem to hold any relevance for her life.

Mike was more satisfied. He found the experience profitable.

He told his counselor that, because of the experience, he resolved to start going back to Sunday Mass regularly again.

Larry found the experience extremely helpful. He discussed with his counselor his problem of talking back to his parents. He also talked about his hope of some day becoming a priest.

Pat found the experience tremendous. She mustered up enough courage to tell her retreat counselor about a personal problem that had been bugging her for over a year now. She resolved to keep in touch with him about it, since he was also her school counselor.

### Cokes and a movie

Four months later, the four friends were having cokes together after a movie. The subject of the retreat came up. The four of them reviewed the effect of the experience on their lives.

Elaine said that she had experienced absolutely no effect in her life as a result of the retreat.

Mike said that he had kept his resolution for three weeks. He finally broke it, however, when some of his buddies began to kid him about getting holy.

Larry admitted that he had become so involved in his school-work and social life that after a month he had completely forgotten the experience.

Pat was last to speak. She said that she had fallen back into her problem a couple of times, but she was now making real progress for the first time. She said that she was still keeping her retreat resolution to keep in touch with her counselor on the problem.

### Stunned amazement

The next Sunday the four young friends went to Mass together. The Gospel for the day was the Parable of the Sower. As the priest read it, the four friends sat in stunned amazement. Each felt that Christ was personally talking to him or her.

Behold, the sower went out to sow. And as he sowed, some seeds fell by the wayside, and the birds came and ate them up. And other seeds fell upon rocky ground, where they had not much earth; and they sprang up at once, because they had no depth of earth; but when the sun rose they were scorched, and because they had no root they withered away. And other seeds fell among thorns; and the thorns grew up and choked them. And other seeds fell upon good ground, and yielded fruit, some

132

a hundredfold, some sixtyfold, and some thirtyfold. He who has ears to hear, let him hear!

Hear, therefore, the parable of the sower. When anyone hears the word of the kingdom, but does not understand it, the wicked one comes and snatches away what has been sown in his heart. This is he who was sown by the wayside. And the one sown on rocky ground, that is he who hears the word and receives it immediately with joy; yet he has not root in himself, but continues only for a time, and when trouble and persecution come because of the word, he at once falls away. And the one sown among the thorns, that is he who listens to the word; but the care of this world and the deceitfulness of riches choke the word, and it is made fruitless. And the one sown upon good ground, that is he who hears the word and understands it; he bears fruit and yields in one case a hundredfold, in another sixtyfold, and in another thirtyfold. Matthew 13:3-9, 18-23.

82 How did this parable act as a radar screen for the students? Which student corresponds to the seed: 1) among thorns, 2) on the wayside, 3) on good soil, 4) on rocky ground?

## 50 CHANGING YOUR LIFE

The secret to keeping resolutions
is know-how, not willpower.

The Parable of the Four Friends brings up the knotty problem of resolutions. Many of us make them, but few of us end up keeping them. Why?

Frequently, the reason is not our lack of willpower to carry them out, but rather our lack of know-how to set them up correctly. Here are some pointers that experts suggest for people who want to carry out resolutions.

1 Decide <u>what</u> needs changing in your life. For example, I should stop cheating; I should stop arguing with my parents; I should get to Mass more often.

2 Decide <u>why</u> this change is needed in your life. For example, cheating can get me into the habit of taking the easy way out; it makes me lazy; it could lead to cheating in bigger things later in my life; it hurts other people whose class rank is lowered because of my dishonesty; it is contrary to Christ and what he stands for. Honesty would make me more self-reliant. It would give me a sense of achievement and self-respect. It is what Christ would do.

3 Decide on a resolution that is both concrete and possible. For example, I will make a sincere effort to be honest during the coming week. This kind of resolution is concrete. It is also

possible, because it covers only a week. Each week it could be renewed. It sometimes helps to write your exact resolution on a piece of paper. On this same sheet of paper you could keep a record of your successes and failures on a day-to-day basis. Some people find that it helps to impose a penalty upon themselves each time they fail.

4 If you can possibly do so, you might discuss your resolution with a counselor whom you trust. Ask him for any suggestions that he might have in helping you to carry it out.

5 Determine and anticipate the things that cause you to cheat. For example, I don't study enough; I fool around too much in class, because I sit with others who cause me to fool around; I don't want others to know that I am not as good as they think I am; I am envious of someone who usually scores higher than I do, and I want to show him up.

6 Renew your resolution and motivation daily. Each night before going to bed take a couple of minutes to do three things: 1) to check yourself on how well you kept the resolution that day, 2) to remind yourself of what you stand to gain or to lose by succeeding or failing, 3) to renew your resolution for the coming day, and to ask God's special help in a short prayer.

83 Why make a resolution for only a week at a time? What is the reason for points two and five above?

photograph by Harold M. Lambert

No longer can people scoff at
miracles. They do happen.


## 51 UNQUESTIONABLE

Closely connected with Christ's parables were his miracles.
First of all, Christ used miracles to get people to listen to him
and to take him seriously. When people saw him heal the sick
and give sight to the blind, they were deeply moved. They realized that there was something unusual about this man. They began to ask him questions.

Second, Christ used miracles to confirm what he told the people. He said, "If you don't believe what I say, believe what I do."

Finally, Christ used miracles to teach the people important
truths about this life and life to come. We will take up this point
in greater detail later.

Let us now take a closer look at miracles, in general, and
Christ's miracles, in particular.

Nobel prize winner

Dr. Alexis Carrel was a top surgeon who won the Nobel prize
for his work in the field of medicine. Among other things, he
demonstrated that certain types of cells can be kept alive forever.

At the peak of his career, Dr. Carrel was an unbeliever. He
doubted the existence of God. He refused to accept Christianity.

But something happened to wipe out his disbelief and to reverse his position on God and Christianity. What made this out-

standing surgeon and Nobel prize winner change his mind? Dr.
Carrel gives the reasons in his book, The Voyage to Lourdes.
This book documents his own personal experience of witnessing
a cure at Lourdes.

The story of Lourdes can be told in a few words. In 1858
a young girl had a profound religious experience concerning
the Virgin Mary. As a result of this experience, a number of
sick people, brought to Lourdes, were cured. Then more and
more people started to come. Now over two million people a
year come to Lourdes.

## Documented

Discussing the cures at Lourdes, the non-Catholic author,
Ruth Cranston makes these comments in her well-known book,
The Miracle of Lourdes.

> The day is past when professional men could scoff at such
> things. Five thousand doctors have banded together in an
> international medical association for the scientific study of
> the cures at Lourdes. They are from many countries: Aus-
> tralia, Argentina, India, Egypt, Turkey, Spain, Sweden,
> England, the United States, and many others. Investigations
> of the cures are as precise and methodical as the analyses
> at any first-class hospital. A Medical Commission of twenty
> distinguished physicians and surgeons of various countries
> passes upon these records before a cure is finally and of-
> ficially declared. When it is declared, you may be sure it
> is authentic and rests on unimpeachable evidence.

> The Medical Bureau at Lourdes has an official file of over
> 1,200 case records of unexplainable cures at Lourdes. These
> records are carefully documented and often include X-ray and
> clinical reports along with doctor's diagnosis and certificates.
> A question automatically arises. With such massive, official
> evidence on record, why do people still doubt or suspend judgment
> about what has taken place at Lourdes? Or why would a man, like
> Dr. Carrel, still doubt in spite of the fact that he saw a miracle
> with his own eyes?

84 How would you be inclined
to answer the above questions,
especially the last one?

## 52  EYEWITNESS

What follows are excerpts from Dr. Alexis Carrel's book,
The Voyage to Lourdes. They describe his journey to Lourdes
and relate what took place while he was there. For professional
reasons, Dr. Carrel changes names and mentions doctors only
by their initials. He refers to himself as Dr. Lerrac (Carrel
spelled backwards).

### At Lourdes

After a long, difficult journey, the train, packed with sick people and invalids, arrived at Lourdes. Lerrac was impressed by
the atmosphere, but he was extremely skeptical about any mirac-
ulous happenings. Speaking to a friend, he said:

"I propose to be entirely objective, " . . . "and I assure you that
if I actually saw one single wound close and heal before my eyes,
I would either become a fanatic believer or go mad. However,
that is not very likely, because I have only had a chance to
examine a few patients with organic diseases. Four of the
cases I saw [on the train] are very interesting. . . .
    "But there is one patient, " Lerrac said, "who is closer to
death at this moment than any of the others. I have already
been called to her bedside several times. Her name is

Marie Ferrand.

"This unfortunate girl is in the last stages of tubercular peritonitis. I know her history. Her whole family died of tuberculosis. . . . Her condition is very grave; I had to give her morphine on the journey. She may die any moment right under my nose. If such a case as hers were cured, it would indeed be a miracle. I would never doubt again; I would become a monk!"

"Take care! Don't be too rash!" said A.B., laughing. "In Lourdes, all the laws of nature are constantly turned upside down."

## At the shrine

Later on, Lerrac tells how Marie Ferrand is carried to the shrine to be bathed in one of the pools there.

A.B., with another volunteer, was carrying a stretcher. On it lay Marie Ferrand.

She lay on her back, all shrunken beneath the dark brown blanket which made a mound over her distended abdomen. Her breath came quick and short. . . .

For a moment, before going to the pool, they lowered the stretcher to the ground. The sick girl was apparently unconscious. Lerrac put his hand on her wrist. Her pulse was more rapid than ever. Her face was ashen. . . .

## At the pool

Marie Ferrand is carried to the pool to be bathed in it. Then she is carried back to where Lerrac is stationed. He examines her and finds no change in her condition. A priest begins the usual prayers for the sick.

The priest was kneeling down, facing the line of patients and the crowds beyond. He lifted his arms and held them out like a cross. . . .

"Holy Virgin, heal our sick," he cried out, . . .

"Holy Virgin, heal our sick," the crowd responded with a cry like the rolling of waves.

"Holy Virgin," intoned the priest, "hear our prayers!"

"Jesus, we love Thee!"

"Jesus, we love Thee!"

140

The voice of the crowd thundered on. Here and there, people held out their arms. The sick half-raised themselves on their stretchers. The atmosphere was tense with expectancy.

Then the priest stood up.

"My brothers, let us lift our arms in prayer!" he called. . . .

Lerrac glanced again at Marie Ferrand. . . .

Something was taking place. He stiffened to resist a tremor of emotion. Standing against the low wall near the stretcher, he concentrated all his powers of observation on Marie Ferrand. . . . Her eyes, so dim before, were now wide with ecstasy as she turned them toward the Grotto. . . .

Suddenly, Lerrac felt himself turning pale. The blanket which covered Marie Ferrand's distended abdomen was gradually flattening out.

"Look at her abdomen!" he exclaimed to M.

M. looked.

"Why yes," he said, "it seems to have gone down. It's probably the folds in the blanket that give that impression."

The bell of the basilica had just struck three. A few minutes later, there was no longer any sign of distension in Marie Ferrand's abdomen.

Lerrac felt as though he were going mad. . . .

Standing beside Marie Ferrand, he watched the intake of her breath and the pulsing at her throat with fascination. The heartbeat, though still very rapid, had become regular.

This time, for sure, something was taking place.

"How do you feel?" he asked her.

"I feel very well," she answered in a low voice. "I am still weak, but I feel I am cured." . . .

Lerrac stood there in silence, his mind a blank. This event, exactly the opposite of what he had expected, must surely be nothing but a dream. . . .

Abruptly, Lerrac moved off. Making his way through the crowd of pilgrims whose loud prayers he hardly heard, he left the Grotto. It was now about four o'clock.

A dying girl was recovering.

Back at the hotel

Lerrac went back to his hotel, forbidding himself to draw any conclusions until he could find out exactly what had happened. . . .

Despite his determination not to draw conclusions, however, Lerrac could not help going over Marie Ferrand's case in his mind and telling himself that with such absolutely unmistakable symptoms as hers, he could not possibly have made a false diagnosis. . . . At half-past seven, he started for the hospital, tense and on fire with curiosity.

The sun had vanished behind the hilltops. In the early-evening quiet, the patients on stretchers or in little carts were being taken back to the hospital; they were singing hymns and <u>Aves</u>.

Arriving at the hospital, Lerrac went straight to the room where Marie Ferrand had been taken to be examined by the Bureau of Medical Records. Lerrac found Marie Ferrand sitting up in bed. "The change was overpowering."

Lerrac, along with two other doctors, examined the girl. Their conclusions were unanimous.

There could be no doubt whatever that the girl was cured. It was, of course, the most momentous thing he had ever seen. It was both frightening and wonderful to see life come pouring back into an organism almost totally destroyed by years of illness.

Here was an indisputable fact; yet it was a fact impossible to reconcile with science. A dying girl had recovered. . . .

To hide his emotion, Lerrac left the room.

> 85 Do you think Lerrac's emotion was one of: joy at the girl's recovery, fear of what the miracle implied, gratitude, or bewilderment? Explain.

Soul in conflict

Later that night Lerrac went for a long walk by himself. A deep conflict was going on within his soul.

Now and then, as Lerrac strode restlessly along the terrace, he heard the muffled voices of the great organs swelling through the night. A passing watchman made the flagstones re-echo beneath his hobnailed boots. From inside the basilica came a sudden burst of full-throated song. A group of Basque pilgrims crowded the portals of the church.

At the threshold, Lerrac stopped. He had to reach a con-

clusion. He was certain of his diagnosis. It was uncontestable
that a miracle had taken place; it was indeed a miracle, a
great one. But was it the hand of God? Some day he would
know. Meanwhile it was safe to say it was a cure; that much
he could guarantee. Yet deep within himself, he felt that was
not all. . . .

He climbed the steps in the glitter of lights and the gleam
of gold, while the organ boomed and a thousand voices chanted.
He sat down on a chair at the back of the church near an old
peasant. For a long time he sat there motionless, his hands
over his face, listening to the hymns.

And this was the prayer he found himself saying:

Gentle Virgin, . . . Thou didst answer my prayers by a
blazing miracle. I am still blind to it, I still doubt. . . .

Take unto Thyself this uneasy sinner with the anxious
frown and troubled heart who has exhausted himself in the
vain pursuit of fantasies. Beneath the deep, harsh warnings
of my intellectual pride a smothered dream persists. Alas,
it is still only a dream but the most enchanting of them all.
It is the dream of believing in Thee and of loving Thee with
the shining spirit of the men of God.

No longer troubled

Slowly, Lerrac walked down the long avenues in the peace-
ful night and crossed the place du Rosaire, bathed in the moon's
milky light.

Absorbed in his prayer, he scarcely felt the fresh night air.
Back in his hotel room again, it seemed to him as though weeks
had gone by since he had left it. He took the big green notebook
from his bag and sat down to write his observations on the final
events of the day. By now it was three o'clock. A pale light in
the east was already breaking through the depths of the night sky.

A new coolness penetrated from the open window. He felt
the serenity of nature entering his soul with gentle calm. All
preoccupations with daily life . . . and intellectual doubts had
vanished.

86 Why do you think Lerrac
found it so hard to believe? Has
Lerrac's essay affected your
own faith in any way?

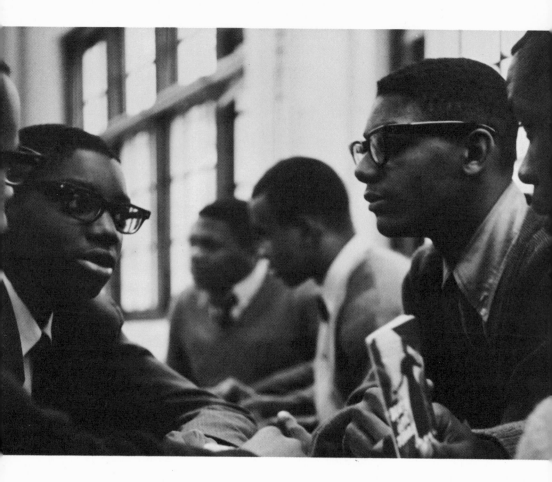

## 53 REACTION

Six students explain why Carrel
still found it hard to believe.


Max: When something remarkable happens, people find themselves in a stupor, and afterwards we tend to doubt the happening
of the event at all. An example can be given from track.

Let's say there is a person who really can't run too well. He
just runs for fun and experience. Let's say this person (me, for
example) runs a mile pretty badly. Then one day he decides he's
going to keep pace with the leaders (which I could never do). Let's
say he finishes with the leaders and comes up with an unbelievable
time. He's not going to believe it, because he's never done it before.
Now, by the time the day is over, he will have talked himself out
of an excellent track time. He'll probably think to himself, "It
must have been a slow heat, and the watches went wrong." (I'm
not saying that he really wants to undo himself, but he can't
bring himself to believe his time.)

This is the same with Dr. Carrel. He sees something, but he
can't bring himself to believe it to be true, because it seems so
impossible.

Martha: If I were a nonbeliever and saw such a miracle, I
probably would do the same as Dr. Carrel did. I probably would
not believe right away. . . . I really don't think that the miracle
was what made him start believing, or even that it was meant to
be. I think it was meant to be a means by which he started praying.

Jeff: The reason Dr. Carrel still finds his experience hard to believe is because of human nature. We have a tendency to doubt anything that doesn't fit into our logical system. Each one of us sets up a system whereby we learn and live. If suddenly we were faced with something that doesn't fit in our logical system, we would probably reject it. This is just what Lerrac (Dr. Carrel) did.

I don't think it stubborn of anyone to doubt the experience that Dr. Carrel claimed to have. I only think it unwise to say that something like this can't exist.

Anton: Lerrac (Carrel) is not alone in his problem. I think that many people, when they see the result of an unknown cause --even in daily life--look for a complicated explanation, while a simple one is staring them in the eye. People seem to think that a simple explanation is not possible or desirable for events that might change the structure of a person's life. . . . It is difficult for us to have faith in something we cannot understand.

Linda: I think he still finds it hard to believe because he is not sure he wants to believe. Believing would mean a complete rethinking of his basic beliefs. It would entail a major change in his life. Not wanting this, he is simply tempted not to believe.

Dan: Even had I been there beside Dr. Carrel, or in his place I do not know what I would have done or thought. I would have been bewildered, perhaps even frightened at first. All in all, I think it would strengthen my faith, but I would not want the miracle to be the center of my faith.

The event probably affected Carrel rather than effected him. I think God would prefer it this way, so that we would have the chance to believe rather than be shown.

> 87 Which of the above com-
> ments do you most agree with?
> least agree with? Why?

146

## 54 NEW ERA

Miracles are signs, announcing
the dawn of a new era in history.

When we pick up the New Testament, we are immediately struck
by the miracles that Christ worked. We see Christ straighten the
bent arm of a cripple. We see him touch the spongy skin of a leper
and make it firm. We see him erase the glassy stare of a blind
man's eyes simply by dabbing them with mud and spit.

The big question is not how Christ worked these miracles (though
we are curious about this), but rather why he worked them. What
point was he trying to make? What was the deeper meaning behind
Christ's miracles?

### Deeper meaning

To understand the deeper meaning behind Christ's miracles,
we must recall that the Old Testament prophets had predicted
that a new era would some day dawn in Israel. For example, the
prophet Isaia said, "Then will the eyes of the blind be opened,
the ears of the deaf be cleared; then will the lame leap like a
stag, then the tongue of the dumb will sing." Isaia 35:5-6.

This is precisely what Christ did. He opened the eyes of the
blind, made the deaf to hear, healed the cripple, and loosed the
tongue of the dumb. Thus, when John the Baptist sent a group of
people to Jesus to ask him if he were the promised one, Jesus
said to them, "Go and bring word to John about all you see and

hear: the blind recover sight, the lame walk, lepers are made clean, the deaf hear, dead men rise again, the humble have the Good News preached to them." Luke 7:22.

### Another way

Christ taught that a new era of history was beginning by yet another way. He did this by showing his power over sin, sickness, and death. Recall that these three evils entered human history as a result of Adam's sin. They had held sway over mankind since that time. By forgiving the sinner, healing the sick, and raising the dead, Christ made it clear that the old era was ending and that a new era was dawning.

### Third way

Finally, Christ taught that his miracles were the signs of a new era in history by yet a third way. He did this by driving demons out of the people. Speaking to the Pharisees about this, Christ said, "If . . . I drive out demons by the Spirit of God, then evidently the kingdom of God [the new era in history] has by now made its way to you." Matthew 12:28.

### Revolutionary truths

Besides using miracles to teach the people that a new era of history was dawning, Christ also used miracles to teach the people important truths about the new era in history. For example, at the wedding reception in Cana, Christ changed water into wine. Also, at an outdoor sermon, Christ fed five thousand people with five loaves and two fishes. Both of these miracles prepared men for the institution of the Eucharist. The Eucharist (Mass) would be the sign of the new era in history. It would also be the means by which Christ would: 1) teach men the meaning behind the new era, and 2) empower them to participate actively in bringing it to its fullness. Christ merely launched the new era; his followers were to carry it to completion.

In brief, Christ worked miracles: 1) to announce the launching of a new era in history, and 2) to teach important truths about this new era.

88 How did miracles announce a new era?

148

## 55 DISBELIEF

Miracles only invite faith;
the door to faith is prayer.

The same icy skepticism that surrounds the miracles at Lourdes also surrounded the miracles of Christ. John 9:1-41.

Many Jews in Christ's time refused to believe in Christ or his miracles, because they were unwilling to set aside their own preconceived notions and ideas. They had their own pet ideas about the new era, which the prophets foretold. They were hoping that the promised Messiah who would launch the new era would be a warrior-king, like David. They expected him to free Israel, in a material sense, from things like political domination by her enemies. They dreamed of a Messiah who would catapult Israel into first place among the nations of the earth.

When Christ tells the people that the new era of history that he is launching is primarily one of spiritual concern, many of them balk. They had in mind a material kingdom, not a spiritual one. They wanted a king who would wear a crown of gold, not a crown of thorns. They were disenchanted. These ideas conflicted with their own personal dreams of power and world domination. Thus they refused to accept Christ. They closed their eyes to his miracles and stopped their ears to his message. Christ said to them:

So the prophecy of Isaiah comes true in their case:
You will listen and listen, but not understand;
You will look and look, but not see.

Because this people's mind is dull;
They have stopped their ears,
And they have closed their eyes. Matthew 13:14-15.

Not automatic

Miracles of themselves do not produce faith. They cannot force us to believe. We are left free to accept or to reject the miracle. Recall the Pharisees who witnessed Christ's cure of the blind man. They refused to believe, even though they had seen the miracle with their own eyes. John 9:1-41.

We are like the Pharisees. If we don't want to believe, no one --not even God--can make us believe.

Miracles can only make us stop and think. They cannot automatically give us faith. Faith will come to us only on our knees in prayer. We saw this in the case of Dr. Carrel. Even after he saw the miracle, he said, "I am still blind to it, I still doubt." Only when he prayed did his intellectual doubts vanish. The door to faith is prayer.

89 Why does Christ make it so hard for us to believe in him?

Only way?

We all know people who have heard about Christ and the Bible, and who refuse to believe either. One such person said, "The only thing that would make me believe is if my best friend came back from the dead and said, 'Jim, I just came back to tell you that life after death is just as Christ and the Bible said it was.'"

The question arises: Would such a person begin to believe or would he find some other excuse for explaining away this new information?

90 How would you answer this last question? How does the parable in Luke 16:19-31 answer this question?

150

Why is the Christian hiding his
light under a cardboard box?

## 56 OVER—OR JUST BEGINNING?

Christ's miracles and parables were the trumpets of a new
world order: a revolution. They were the alarm clocks of history,
jarring men from beds of apathy. They were the first shafts of
daylight piercing the night sky. They were the heralds of a new day.
Christ triggered a revolution. His miracles burst in upon the
world of human evil and unconcern like a bomb.
Christ healed the blind. Behind this miracle, however, was
a deeper meaning. It was a sign to all men--to open their eyes
to the bright light of a new day. Christ unplugged the ears of the
deaf. It, too, was a sign--that all men should open their ears to
what he had to say. Christ forgave sinners. Again, it was a sign--
that all men should undergo a change of heart and begin new lives.

Shattering

Christ's miracles were sensational, shattering, and alarming.
Their purpose was to awaken the world--to set in motion what
Christ dubbed the kingdom of God.
And what was this kingdom? It was a new world order, in
which all men would become brothers--and treat each other as
brothers. It was the beginning of a new world order in which
love would replace hate, concern would replace unconcern,
light would replace darkness, and life would replace death.

Let it ring

The battle cry, "thy kingdom come," was to ring out and ring out. Christ told men to shout it from housetops, paint it in big letters on weather-beaten walls, sing it around night campfires, chant it in the temples, tattoo it on their hearts. But more important, Christ told men to do something about it.

The healing miracles that shattered the windows of time and crumbled the walls of history were now to be continued by men-- not in a sensational way, but by the new miracle of life and love that Christ transplanted into their feeble minds and bodies. They were to be men on fire with the Spirit of Christ.

No longer a stranger

The hungry man, the thirsty woman, the naked child. These would now find a brother, where before they saw only a stranger passing them like a ship in the night.

I was hungry and you gave me to eat;
I was thirsty and you gave me to drink;
I was a stranger and you took me in;
naked and you covered me;
sick and you visited me;
I was in prison and you came to me . . .
as long as you did it for one of these,
the least of my brethren, you did it for me.
Matthew 25:35-40.

This was the revolution. This was the sign. This was the new miracle of history that was to renew the face of the earth. "Send forth your Spirit, and they will be re-created." The face of the earth will never look the same again.

I was hungry and you shared your lunch with me;
I was thirsty and you gave me half your coke;
I forgot my jacket and you loaned me your best sweater;
I was different and you told the others not to make fun of me;
I was sick and you explained the homework to me;
I was grounded for the weekend and you watched TV with me;
As long as you did it for one of these,
the least of my brethren, you did it for me.

152

This revolution goes on. Or does it? Modern Christians are called to be miracle workers--amazing the world with their love and concern. They are to be lightning bolts and thunderclaps. But are they? Why are so many of them hiding their lights under cardboard boxes?

Christians, where are you? What's wrong with you? Has the spirit of Christ gone out of you as the air leaves a punctured tire? Or didn't you ever understand what Christianity was all about? What is your excuse? Who will answer? Is the revolution Christ started over or is it just beginning?

91 How would you answer the above questions?

Being a Christian is a question of
life service, not lip service.


## 57 ACTION

Christ's message was revolutionary. It challenged people; it
challenged institutions; it challenged the establishment. "Feed the
hungry, help the sick, befriend the stranger"--these were concrete things. They were calls to action. Christ made it perfectly
clear that being a Christian was not a question of lip service,
but of life service.

Christ intentionally expressed his call to action in a concrete
but sketchy form: feed the hungry, help the sick, befriend the
stranger. In doing so, he did not restrict it to any age group or
period of history. He wants us to apply it to our own lives and
times. We saw one way to do this in the previous reading. Here
are two other ways to apply it to our times. Read, discuss, and
evaluate each application.

First way

I was hungry and you put a photograph of me holding an empty
plate on your bulletin board.

I was thirsty and you organized a discussion group to explore
and study my wretched condition.

I was a stranger, a member of an immigrant minority group in
your country, and you read an article in class about me.

I was without sufficient clothes and you gathered statistics to

154

prove how much worse off I was than you.

I was sick and you wrote an article about my disease in your school paper.

I was in prison and you debated in class whether prisons helped or hindered in rehabilitating me.

As long as you did it for one of these, the least of my brethren, you did it for me.

92  What is your reaction to these applications? Would you say they are what Christ had in mind?

Another version

I was hungry and you initiated a canned-food drive in your school to help feed me.

I was thirsty and you contributed to the missions to help me to dig wells and pipe water.

I was naked and you canvassed the neighborhood to find used clothes for me.

I was a stranger and you gave up your Saturday mornings to help me learn to read your language.

I was sick and you volunteered to help at the hospital so that the nurses might have more time to care for me.

I was in prison and you organized a group to sing carols to me on Christmas to show that you cared for me.

As long as you did it for one of these, the least of my brethren, you did it for me.

93  How do these applications differ from the previous ones? Within what context does Christ present the above corporal works of mercy? See Matthew 25:1-46.

# CHAPTER 4

# NEIGHBORHOOD WORLD

"A place for every man, but
every man in his place."

## 58 PEOPLE BEHIND WALLS

The Berlin Wall is an affront to human dignity. All of us become
a bit angry when we think about it. It is hard for us to understand
how a modern nation can treat people in such an inhuman way.

Yet, right here in America we have built our own Berlin Walls.
True, we did not build them out of concrete or barbed wire. But
we might just as well have.

For years we have walled off large segments of our society from
the mainstream of American life. We didn't do this so much out of
hatred as we did out of utter stupidity and gross insensitivity to the
plight and need of our neighbors. While we took pride that in America "there is a place for every man," we might have blushed had
someone also pointed out that this was true "providing every man
stayed in his place."

Now things are beginning to change. We are starting to learn
more about our neighbor. And as our stupidity decreases, hopefully our sensitivity will increase.

In the remainder of this essay and in the four to follow, author
John Travis (in "Contributors All") tries·to enlighten us about five
minority groups and how they have contributed to our country, in
spite of our treatment of them. Hopefully, his brief survey will
give us a deeper appreciation of these neighbors and spur us on
to seek a better acquaintance with them. Travis begins his survey
with a look at the original American, the Indian.

Not so savage

To many people the word <u>savage</u> brings to mind an American
Indian. Few know that the Iroquois Confederacy represented an
established democratic society that was already 200 years old when
our Constitution was written. Jefferson openly acknowledged his
debt to the Iroquois' example. Notice your food tomorrow. You
can thank the Indian for much of it. Four-sevenths of our foodstuffs
are derived from plants cultivated by American Indians. It is well
known that corn grown by Indians helped on more than one occa-
sion to save the early settlers from starvation. Not so well known
is the fact that the Indian also gave us the squash, lima bean,
tomato, potato, and watermelon. Add to that list the peanut, the
valuable peanut, grown by the Indian and put to a hundred uses by
a Negro scientist. How many lives have been saved by quinine and
cocaine? Both were gifts from our Indian friends. According to
construction men, tall structures, such as the Empire State Building, would not be possible without the ability of certain Indian
steel construction workers to work comfortably at great heights.

Great men

Great Indians abound in our history. Sequoia was the first man
known to have <u>invented</u> an alphabet, a feat that usually takes cen-
turies of slow development. Benjamin Harrison helped write the
Oklahoma constitution, and Johnston Murray was governor of that
state. Charles Curtis was a senator from Kansas and a Vice President of the United States. Will Rogers, a well-known twentieth
century American, boasted of his Indian blood. Maria Tallchief
is known throughout the world as a prima ballerina, and Jim Thorpe
is one of the most famous athletes of all time. In spite of small
numbers, liquidation, and systematic exclusion, the American
Indian has given us priceless possessions.

94 What facts surprised you
most in the above brief report?
Half of the 600,000 red Americans lived on "ghetto" reservations. Is this good or bad?

## 59 JEWISH NEIGHBORS

John Travis reports on the contribution of Jewish Americans.

The first Jews arrived on this continent in 1654, a group of 23
fleeing persecution in Brazil. Despite persecution, discrimination,
and sometimes expulsion, they established themselves as invalu-
able members of American society. Many important businesses
grew from their small retail enterprises, among them Gimbel's
in New York City. One West Coast businessman, Levi Strauss,
gave his name to the famous Levis, a type of trousers popular
throughout the land. The entire American labor movement owes
an incalculable debt to two garment workers' unions formed and
led by Jewish immigrants. They paved the way for many ad-
vances in labor-management negotiations and social action, including health and welfare programs and unemployment com-
pensation. Two of the early leaders of these unions, David
Dubinsky and Sidney Hillman, were guiding spirits in the development in this country of recognition of the rights of the working-
man. Jewish leadership has been highly visible in the fight for
equal rights for all Americans.

Standouts

A glance at almost any occupational area shows that, among
those who stand out, the proportion of Jews is far greater in re-
lation to their actual numbers than those in other groups. In

science, Einstein leads a long list that includes Dr. Jonas Salk. In law [in 1969], Brandeis, Cardozo, Frankfurter, and Fortas have been or are members of the Supreme Court. Adolph Ochs and Joseph Pulitzer are two of our foremost journalists. In music, to name Leonard Bernstein and Vladimir Horowitz is to mention only two of an almost incredible number. In the entertainment field the list that includes George S. Kaufman, Jerome Kern, George Gershwin, Irving Berlin, Danny Kaye, Kirk Douglas, and Benny Goodman seems unending. If your interest is modern literature, you have read Herman Wouk and Irving Stone. The Jewish people do not have to justify their stake in the United States.

95 Numerically, Jews stand out in occupational areas. Do you think this fact feeds prejudice against them? If someone is prejudiced against you, does this spur or stifle your competitive spirit? Explain.

John Travis reports on Oriental
American contributions.


## 60  ORIENTAL BROTHERS

One group to which the popular mind seems to give little attention is the Oriental. However, United States history records that
the Oriental is beyond doubt an integral part of our national development. Although not a slave, he was like the Negro brought
to this continent to provide cheap labor and has remained to become a valuable citizen. From the start, the remarkable skill
of the Japanese in farming made them desirable as agricultural
workers, but feared as competitors. Because of his success as a
farmer, he was the target of legislation that severely restricted
his ability to acquire land. Despite this discrimination, the contributions of Japanese farmers to the agricultural development of
the West are great indeed. Only two examples are needed to es-
tablish the point. Swampy areas that native Americans considered
worthless the Japanese managed to drain and convert into productive potato farms. In the San Joaquin Valley, on land also thought
to be not suited for agriculture, they struggled patiently for years,
and, through application of skillful farming techniques, turned
the valley into a veritable garden spot. Their ability to make such
land productive has benefited the entire country. If an educated
populace is an asset to a country, the Japanese have certainly done
their part. At one time, and it may still be true, they had the high-
est percentage of students enrolled in college of any ethnic group
in California.

## Leaders

In addition to their other gifts, the Oriental immigrant groups have given us many leaders in scholarship, art, and government. T. D. Lee and Chen Ning Yang shared the 1957 Nobel Prize in physics. Jui Hsin Wang is a noted chemist. Others who have distinguished themselves are James Wong Howe, cinematographer and Dong Kingman, artist. Hiram L. Fong and Daniel K. Inouye, senators, from Hawaii, have been prominent in political affairs and government. A noted actor is Sessue Hayakawa, and S. I. Hayakawa is a world-famous semanticist.

96  What historical similarity is there between black and Oriental Americans? In what areas of industrial production do the Japanese excel?

John Travis focuses in on some
Afro-American contributions.

## 61 BLACK COMMUNITY

Between 1619 and 1864, five to 10 million Africans were brought
to this country. It is impossible to believe that this would have occurred had their labor not been valuable. Think of the contribution
to the country's economy made by this group! Without them, the
agricultural economy of the South (based on tobacco, indigo, rice,
and cotton), could not have attained the influence and prosperity
that it enjoyed. Had the Negro given nothing other than his labor,
his contribution, though shameful to the white, should have endeared
him to the nation. But it is not only as field hands that Negroes
served their country. Many became mechanics, artisans, and river
boat pilots. For proof of his value, it is necessary only to recall
that in every crisis, efforts were made to enlist Negro support,
often with promises that were unfulfilled when the crisis had passed.

Prominent men

Even in the days of slavery there were prominent Negroes, among
them Benjamin Banneker, mathematician, surveyor, and mechanical
genius, the explorers Estevanico and Jean DuSable, founder of Chicago,
and Martin Delany, explorer, doctor, editor, and scientist. A bottle-
neck in the shoe industry was broken by inventor Jan Matzeliger, who
developed a lasting machine when veteran shoemakers said it was impossible.

In the Civil War years, Negroes prominent in government service included P. B. S. Pinchback and Henry Garnet. Robert Smalls, a Civil War hero, became a United States congressman and Hiram Revels was a senator.

In our times we are the fortunate beneficiaries of the achievements of Negro scientists prominent in the field of medicine. Among them are Daniel H. Williams, first doctor to operate successfully on the heart, and Charles R. Drew, one of the outstanding young scientists who, through their research findings and experiments, made possible the successful Red Cross blood plasma program that saved many lives in World War II. In the field of scholarship there are John Hope Franklin, historian, William Hastie, teacher, judge, and governor of the Virgin Islands, and Charles S. Johnson, sociologist and university professor. In any field one examines there are outstanding Negroes: Mathew Henson, first man to reach the North Pole; William Grant Still, composer; Paul Williams, architect; Thurgood Marshall, Supreme Court justice. Even this short list helps to indicate our debt to the Negro, and we have not mentioned the familiar names in the performing arts, sports, and other fields.

97 Why aren't we more aware of black contributions in the field such as science? What fact makes black contributions in these areas even more remarkable? Where are blacks now making their greatest contribution on the American scene?

## 62 MEXICAN-AMERICANS

John Travis explores the contribution of Mexican-Americans.

A survey of the Southwest reveals our debt to Mexican-Americans.
That vast area of the country is enlivened through their heritage of
names, architecture, and music. Not so obvious is the debt we owe
them for their contributions to the economic foundations of the
country. As with many other groups, they were a valuable source
of labor. It is owing in large part to their labor that some of the
rich farmlands of the West were developed. And what about our
cattle industry, which we celebrate in song and story and which has
become of great importance to the nutrition of Americans as well
as to their economic health and colorful traditions? It was Mexican-
Americans who taught the early settlers how to herd long-horned
cattle and to use the horned saddle and the branding iron. In short,
they helped to make the cattle industry possible. Even the word
cowboy is of Spanish derivation, as are lariat (which Mexican-
Americans taught us to use), corral, pinto, bronco, and rodeo.

Other contributions

In addition, they opened up mining in the West, and the whole
world is aware of what the mines of the West have brought in riches
to this country. Mexican-Americans introduced the slope-sided
pan to early seekers for gold. The economic life of the United
States would certainly be poorer without their contributions.

From among Mexican-Americans have come leaders. Today, for example, Eligio de la Garza and Henry B. Gonzalez are members of the House of Representatives from Texas. Dennis Chavez was for many years a member of Congress from New Mexico. Today, Cesar Chavez, the labor leader of depressed agricultural workers, has furnished an example of the best in American tradition: pride, compassion, and determination in the face of odds. The right of the Mexican-American to full citizenship has been amply paid. The debt belongs to the country.

Combat heroes

There should be no need to dwell on what each group has done when this nation is at war. The casualty lists show that every group has given of its best. Even while most Negroes were still slaves, over 5,000 Negro troops served in the American Revolution. Jews, who numbered only about 1,500 of the population at that time, furnished three colonels and many officers of lesser rank. Indians who used their native language to confound the enemy during World War II have become a legend, and the Nisei who composed the 442nd Regimental Combat Team made a record any group might envy. If there be any doubters, let them review a list of those upon whom Medals of Honor have been conferred. On it are such names as Rodriquez, Kouma, Miyamura, Hirohi, Cohn, and Chiquito, along with Cooper, Daly, and Smith. No group has a monopoly on service or courage.

98 What facts surprised you most in this brief report on the Mexican-American? Select one of the people mentioned in the previous essays and do further research on him. Report your findings back to the class.

## 63 A BLACK TEEN SPEAKS OUT

Note: The following essay was written by a student (he submitted it as a term paper) at St. Ignatius College Prep, Chicago. Except for the name of the student in the first line of the essay, not a word or a mark of punctuation was changed. Subtitles, alone, were added.

If teachers or students find it hard to believe that this is the work of a black sophomore, then those teachers and students should feel chastened and humbled. It is a sign that they underrate the depth, ability, and articulateness of a significant segment of young people--and black young people, in particular.

"Hey, King."
"What?"
"Did ya hear about that colored guy gettin' his ass kicked over in Gage Park yesterday?"

"Nope. What happened?"

"He was messin' around over there and a bunch of white guys beat 'im up. Boy, was it ever funny!"

The above is an excerpt from the typical kind of dialogue I am involved in with a white teen-ager in my room from time to time. He is an enigma insofar as he kids and jokes around about racial issues, yet is seemingly dead serious when he says, "We don't want no black guys in our neighborhood. We're gonna get rid of all of 'em." However, he is one of the exceptions. As a rule, most of the white kids who might be labeled prejudiced confine their thoughts to their heads, and never talk about it to a black kid. Whether they talk about it with other white kids in the room I'm not sure.

## Not prejudiced

I feel the reason these teen-agers are the way they are is that they are confronted by group pressure, which seems to play a most significant role in the life of an adolescent. Most of them if not all of them live in all-white areas, surrounded by other kids who have misconceptions about black people and also by older white people who probably never even knew a black person. I think this is the primary reason most of them have a hard time breaking away from such ill thinking. Even though here in school there are black kids who are no more militant or rowdy than the most sissified white kid, some white students absolutely will not accept them. They think all blacks like to fight. These kids are too young to have had any real experiences with black people, so they simply believe the fallacies of their elders.

To my way of thinking, these kids are not actually prejudiced. It is merely that they are afraid and above all, ignorant of the facts. I can understand how it might feel to come to the realization that your parents are racist, that despite how much you love them, they are wrong. Yet is it sane to let such ideas flourish in your own mind, when you know they are false? Is it humanly right to let sentimentality obstruct your responsibility toward humanity? I don't think so, and I'm sure most of those labeled as being prejudiced don't really think so. Mainly they are too cowardly to take that first step.

Certainly an attitude of this sort can have adverse effects on his family, friends, and society. If members of your family are just as disillusioned as you are, they rely on the outlook of each other as justification for what they think. In this way, each mem-

ber of the family encourages everyone else to do the same.
Among friends there is an "in" group and an "out" group. If you
want to belong to the "in" group, you'd better conform and be
like the rest of them. If you don't, you're a social outcast. They
look upon you as a traitor.

Yet if everyone did his individual share in dispelling these
myths, there would be no worry.

### Big opportunity

This is where I think the white kids at St. Ignatius have a priv-
ilege that many other white kids don't have--they can talk to black
teens, work with black teens, have recreation with black teens, and
conclusively find out that they are human, and for the most part, just
like everyone else. Most assuredly there are cultural differences
such as the type of clothing they wear and the ghetto dialect they
might use, but the white kids will find out that these are superficial
trademarks, which do not project the kind of character he has. If
the white kids will give an honest appraisal of situations and really
try to be open-minded, certainly they will make progress.

This is not to say, however, that all black people they come
into contact with will be "great guys." Certainly, there is ill will
on both sides of the color line, and there are black bigots just as
well as there are white ones. This is why being objective in judging
a person is the most accurate way of determining character. By no
means is color a determining factor.

### All neighbors

Didn't Christ say, "Whatsoever you do unto the least of my brethren, that you do unto me"? Didn't he preach the doctrine of love
towards thy fellow man? We are all confined to this earth. We all
rely on each other to survive. Therefore, in the universal sense
of the word, we are all neighbors. The students here, being Christians, certainly should advocate the teachings of Christ.

### Hope in youth

It would be an idealistic hypothesis to say that one day all prejudice will be eliminated. Perhaps it won't. But the youth of today,
who are the adults of tomorrow, must strive to be as perfect as
human nature will allow.

One fact which helps to verify my statement that most of youth who might be considered prejudiced are this way because of environment and group pressure is the attitude college youth have towards the racial crisis. Away from home, they are exposed to a more liberal education and can give their true opinion, ask questions, and fraternize with all types of people without fear of reprisal from their parents and people in the neighborhood. They can go out for themselves and find out where it's at--where truth is at.

### Begin with yourself

Admittedly not an erudite scholar or man of the world, I must admit that I am honest with myself, and when I am trying to solve a problem, I really open my mind to suggestions and ideas. Therefore, my suggestion to other young adults who want to reduce and indeed eliminate this problem of disillusionment in their lives, is to primarily and firstly work for change within yourself. The fact of the matter is, you can never learn too much about other people. And in order to work for change within yourself, you've got to be open-minded, objective, and analytical. Reading is a great help, and there is a sundry collection of books on race, by both white and black authors. Once you feel you are prepared to defend what you believe, then you go out to make converts. You try to sell your ideas to your brother or sister, and perhaps your parents, even though they are probably over the hill and too set in their ways to change. Having discussion with an integrated group at times is also profitable.

Change isn't easy, but it is our quest.

99 What struck you most about this boy's attitude and viewpoint of the race problem? On what point do you most agree with him?

A high-school student reflects
prejudice among Christians.

## 64 PAST NIGHTMARES?

Witch-burnings and inquisitions are nightmares from the distant past, but there are still many thousands today with this type
of mentality: "Church Bombed." "Ushers Exclude Negro from
Church."

Modern Christians pride themselves on being enlightened. Yet,
today, extremism still reigns under the guise of religious fervor.
Lord, many of your people, supposedly acting on your behalf, exclude others from your houses of worship. Men claiming to speak
for you inflame the passions of others. The masses differentiate
one man from another. Where is our Christian era going? How
can men actually hate in the name of love?

God, in your wisdom, save your people from what we are doing
to ourselves. Give us light to see each other as brothers.

"For you too were once aliens in the land of Egypt." Leviticus
19:34.

100 Explain the statement,
"men actually hate in the name
of love." Do you think Christian
attitudes toward the race question
are changing for the better?

Irene Wray in "Experiment in
Brotherhood" describes an experiment that led to action.

## 65 INVOLVEMENT

It's a big world with much wrong with it that needs to be put
right. But there does not seem to be any starting place. Young
people charged with idealism often find it hard to decide where to
begin. . . . Susan Johnson, a high school student of Sacramento,
California, was one of these young people.

. . . Susan joined various do-good groups, but nothing seemed
to satisfy her. She could never see enough progress. The world
stayed the same. Then one day last spring, she received a letter
that gave her hope. . . .

The letter began, "Congratulations! You have been chosen to
be one of 60 teens to participate in a pilot project which will bring
together youth representatives of various ethnic and religious
groups, so that you may become friends as you learn about the
backgrounds, heritages, and cultures of each other. You will look
for answers to the problems of differences among us, and to problems of poverty and discrimination."

". . . The first meeting was held in a downtown coffee house.
Ten Jews, ten Chinese, ten Mexican-Americans, ten Japanese,
ten Negroes, and ten Caucasians . . . were there."

. . . Susan was shocked by the bitterness apparent in some of
the teenagers' comments. . . . Some of the young people took the
view that brotherhood was patently impossible, that this project
was doomed to failure. But . . . by the time the meeting broke up,

172

the group had formulated plans for a tour of the slum area, a visit to a Confucian center, to a Jewish temple, a Jewish home, and an exploration of the Mexican way of life . . . They would also meet with the leaders of Oak Park's predominantly Negro community. They found a name that reflected their positive approach: Youth Explores Sacramento (YES).

## Mexican-Americans

"I had never been inside a Catholic church," Susan said, "so I was glad of the opportunity. The one we visited serves Spanish-speaking people. Father Kenny told us that all masses are read in Spanish. . . . He said the fact that Mexican-Americans cling to their own traditions and customs both helps and hinders them. Their identity is strengthened, and their feeling of self-worth enhanced by such things as celebration of the Mariachi Mass (worship with Latin American music). But their insistence on speaking Spanish results in poor performance in the English-speaking schools, he said."

Next, YES members boarded a bus for a trip into the delta area, where the farmlands are among the richest in the world, and where the slums are hopeless. Many Mexican-American farmworkers eke out an existence here. They had lost out to automation.

## Jewish-Americans

"In groups of ten, we visited Jewish homes the next week," Susan said. "Here we learned the meaning of Hannukah, the mezuzah on the door, the history of kosher. Our Jewish hosts told us that there wasn't much obvious discrimination against them today . . . except for occasional name calling. But they feel accepted in the community and are determined to help other minority groups find their places in the sun."

They also attended an invitational service at the Temple B'Nai Israel. Cantor Eli Cohn answered questions like: "Can your rabbi get married?" "What is your feeling toward Israel?" "Why has the stereotype of 'cheap Jew' spread around the world?" "How could the world have prevented Hitler's mass extermination of the Jews?" Susan said, "We came to the conclusion that Hitler's program could have been prevented by understanding and knowledge. People were ignorant of the true Jewish customs and beliefs, so they were only too ready to believe false stories that circulated through Germany."

## Afro-Americans

At the Women's Civic Improvement Club in Oak Park, the discussion centered on employment problems, discrimination in housing, and dangers inherent in ghetto life. Solutions posed were support of the Job Corps program and support of a proposal that local businessmen make an effort to hire at least one member of a minority group. Busing students out of the area into an integrated school is already being done.

"We talked about the history courses taught in our schools, which don't show a true picture of the minority groups' contributions to the development of our country," Susan said.

After each exploration into the different areas of Sacramento, YES members met in cluster sessions, discussed what they had learned, and recorded their impressions on huge sheets of newsprint. These impressions were then shared with all 60 members, and ideas for improvement were listed.

## Oriental-Americans

"I had never been inside a Confucian church, either," said Susan. "The first thing we learned there was that it isn't a church, and Confucianism isn't a religion. The building is a social hall and a school where the Chinese language and history are taught. Confucianism is a philosophy of life, and we were told it is practiced widely in Chinese families today. Its tenets are humility, benevolence, and virtue."

Buddhism was explained, and Japanese customs discussed. A kimono was modeled by a Japanese-American girl, and Japanese food was served.

"We learned about the 'containment camps' of the United States during World War II into which thousands of Japanese-Americans were herded. They lost their homes, their businesses, everything. We decided that such a thing must never happen again to any United States citizen."

Now that YES participants had explored their community and had become aware of some of the needs of the people, they felt that they could begin to try to understand brotherhood, to answer the question, "Is brotherhood the impossible dream?"

"We defined brotherhood as being concern, first," Susan said. "Also, it is respect and acceptance. It's freedom from interracial barriers. It is recognition of personal worth, with de-emphasis of ethnic background. We learned that brotherhood

174

starts with self-understanding."

To achieve brotherhood, YES members realized that groups must communicate on a broad scale, that understanding must be translated into action in the school and in the community.

. . . "My new friends wear labels," Susan observed, "and I have learned that I, too, have a label. Minority groups think of me as a WASP (white Anglo-Saxon protestant). I know that they feel more comfortable with each other than with me, but I hope this will change. I have learned many things from them: that Negroes don't like to be called colored people; that prejudice provides a focus for one's own shortcomings; that discrimination hurts; that all of these kids feel pulled and pushed by the demands of their own ethnic cultures and the world outside. I have learned that they are most admirable.

"I am glad I was chosen to work with them. I feel humble and inadequate for the task, but I will do my best."

### Action program

Mrs. Bette Brill, . . . who has been active in YES since it began, had this to say:

"The YES program, which began as a quest for self-knowledge and community understanding, has grown into a true experiment in brotherhood. It's an action program.

"Teenagers in YES work in Head Start programs, with blind children, with the handicapped, in hospitals, and in day camps. Some gave as many as four hours a day during summer months. Some became buddies in the Society for the Blind's buddy system. Here they helped in classes for calisthentics, dancing, grooming, carpentry, eating skills--even bowling!

"YES kids worked at an orphanage, a settlement house, a well-baby clinic, the YWCA, and in the Youth Opportunity Center.

"The main thing is, they're involved. This program has reinforced their individuality. They are capable of communicating outside their own group. They have a sense of self-worth as they go about the business of helping others. They are building a better world, because they have become better persons through understanding."

101 Have you ever been involved in a program similar to YES? What opportunities for such involvement are available in your community?

## 66 POVERTY NEIGHBORHOODS

> In "What It Means To Be Poor"
> Elizabeth Mulligan describes
> the tragedy of poverty.

There comes a time when children wake up to the fact that our society harbors the rich and the poor, and then the pressing question arises to which they must have an answer: "Which are we? Are we rich or poor?"

When I was first faced with the query some years ago, I tried to explain that we were "comfortable" and belonged in that vast middle class where most Americans find themselves.

"I think we must be poor," contradicted my son, "because I don't have everything I want."

What my youngsters needed, I decided, was an object lesson in poverty. So one day the four of us scrambled into our . . . red Oldsmobile, and I drove to the other side of town.

Driving slowly through the narrow, hole-filled dirt streets, I pointed out the crumbling shacks in which people lived. Along the roads open gutters oozed raw sewage that fouled the air. Ragged children played listlessly on plots of ground grassed only with debris and junk.

My daughters seemed to be properly affected by the squalor around them, and feeling rather satisfied with myself, I ventured to say, "Now this is what being poor is."

My son braced himself in the seat and sputtered, "It could mean they're just lazy. They could get to work and clean up this mess. And they could paint their houses."

"They're poor," I explained. "They're so poor they don't have enough money to buy paint."

At that moment we approached an aged shack that couldn't have had more than two rooms. A leaning outside toilet was supported by two pieces of timber wedged against either side. But between the tumble-down shack and the precariously pitched toilet was an automobile. Yes . . . it was [an] . . . Oldsmobile, and it was red!

> 102 If you were the mother, how would you answer her son's question?

### Too young

"Who's poor?" boomed my son.

They were too young, of course, to understand the psychology that links repression and impulsive splurge buying. I felt a sense of defeat in not being able to explain it to them. A final incident added to our frustration, and yet perhaps is the key to our understanding the problem.

"Something hit me!" my son suddenly yelled. On the floor of the car lay a small rock, and peering at us from behind a building were three scowling boys. One of them wiggled his fingers from his nose in farewell as we quickly rolled up the car window and headed out of the area. My son wailed, "Do they have to be mean just because they're poor?"

> 103 How would you answer this question?

### Something more

. . . To many people poverty still means the lack of money and that phase of destitution we can see. It is evident in poor housing, in unkempt streets and alleys, in sullen faces, and in aimless feet. But much more is involved in the condition of poverty than in this visible evidence.

Poverty is also the lack of education. It is the fact that a certain class of people do not have the necessary skills or training to take advantage of employment possibilities. Poverty is being sick often because of unsanitary conditions and unhealthful practices, and in staying sick longer because of the lack of ability

178

and money to cope with illness. Poverty is not just one hardship or one misery, but a miserable combination of problems and situations that must be endured all at one time and all the time.

In fact, social researchers have come to believe that a distinct poverty culture exists, an identifiable personality that is common to the very poor into which they are born and from which they are unlikely to grow without considerable help.

There seems to be an internal insufficiency among the under-privileged that permeates their character: that makes helpless-ness a way of life; that breeds despair and bitterness and affects the way they see and think . . . and the way they do not hope.

. . . New studies made of the poverty-stricken, and fresh insight gained by social research, point up one significant fact: the present poverty in the United States amounts to more than the misfortune of individuals who can be helped by direct assistance. Poverty is, rather, a whole complex of interrelated problems which there is little hope of solving unless they are attacked at their deeply rooted source. To be poor is not simply to be deprived of the material things of this world. Poverty is being part of a hopeless existence, a futile way of life . . . shut out, rejected, frightened, discouraged and defeated. These are the people who know what poverty is all about.

> 104 In your own words explain what the author means by the statement: "Poverty is a com-bination of problems and situ-ations."

Young and poor

The area in which the culture of poverty is most painful to witness is among the young people. Not long ago the Department of Labor published a study called "One Out of Three" which revealed that only one out of three of our young American males is judged fit for military service. The majority of the others are rejected because of "mental reasons." In this case, "mental" does not refer to psychiatric conditions but to the fact that the rejectees are young men in our society who do not measure up to a sixth grade education. More than that, the study continued to show that most of these young men are from families which have long been on public relief.

In the training camps now in existence as part of our War
on Poverty, four major skills are being drilled into these youth.
They are reading, writing, arithmetic . . . and speech. You
might ask, why speech?

"These young people lack the ability to understand others, and
they can't express themselves," said Sargent Shriver. "They do
not understand directions and so they are unable to follow directions. They appear to be foreigners in a society of common,
everyday situations."

Why?

. . . A study of the family patterns of the poor furnishes much
information, and it shows that the husband in the low-class home
plays a very small role in family life. He seems to feel that his
responsibility is to provide "a living" if he can, but that he should
be free to come and go at will. As a result, the wife assumes
most of the responsibilities of the home, including that of rear-
ing the children.

Frequently it is the husband who becomes an economic burden.
Lower-class women have more success in finding and holding
jobs than do their husbands. Therefore, some women consider it
an economic risk to marry or to stay married, and this condition is at the bottom of the widely prevalent female-based
homes in the slum areas. Usually such households consist of
one or more women, often related, with a setup commonly accepted in which the women have a succession of temporary
partners. And the children of these families see sex relationships that are based on almost anything except love.

105 Why are lower-class wom-
en more able to find and hold
jobs than their husbands? What
problem does this create?

Educational famine

Another area of study involved the educational performance of
the children in low-income groups. These children appear to be
retarded in subject matter, in comprehension, and in experience
situations. While it is true that many conditions contribute to
the educational famine of these children, it is perhaps the parents who affect their lack of achievement most. Often there is

no motivation at all that might encourage a child to succeed in school. The child's vocabulary is pitifully meager. He has never had the opportunity of hearing a variety of words. He can't communicate. He probably has never seen his parents reading a book, and most likely has never held one in his hands before entering school. Parents do not encourage questions from their children because they themselves do not know the answers. There is simply no incentive for learning . . . no reason why they should try.

106  To what extent can schools make up for home defects?

## Treated like dirt

. . . In the field of health, the poor generally behave differently than any other group in our society. . . .

When they do seek help they are more likely to go to sub-professionals and even to "quacks." They are inclined to feel that if they do seek the care of reputable doctors they will receive a "different" type of treatment than the better-off patients.

. . . The use of free clinics made available to the destitute is not utilized as much as commonly thought. The crowds seen there are usually not the very poor, and those who do venture to public clinics are not happy about the results. They feel that better educated people are contemptuous of them. As one woman said, "Them folks act like I'm dirt." So, feeling that they have been poorly treated, and often not really understanding the advice given, they are less likely to follow instructions, and the results of their clinic visits are, "It didn't do me no good."

## Two eggs and a basket

. . . In the field of consumer practices, one critic concludes that the poor are poor because of irrational buying. They tend to buy two or three eggs instead of a dozen; a basket of coal instead of a ton, and these daily dribbles make living costs higher than if supplies were bought in larger quantities. It is true, of course, but it must be remembered that a small income has to be divided into smaller amounts than a large income. Low-income families cannot take advantage of lower-priced quantity buying. . . .

In the category of durable goods, automobiles, television sets and radios prove to be the greatest temptation to poor-class consumers. To most of society these items are part of the standard package of an American household, but to the poor they are status symbols. Since they are denied access to other forms of social status they tend to pay more for this type of goods than their meager earnings allow.

Some surveys indicate that low-income shoppers do not get the best values in their purchases. Merchandise in poor neighborhoods, it is asserted, is usually inferior, and prices are generally higher than in middle-class markets. And, since the poor are not educated to value-buying, they are liable to leave the store with poor bargains and high bills.

107 Why are high-priced cars and TV sets a great temptation to the poor?

## Unrest and protest

. . . The biggest reason why more attention is now being given to poverty problems is that social ills arising from concentrations of the poor in big cities are becoming worrisome . . . and a more costly burden . . . to the remainder of the population. The protest movements of the Negroes have created a new urgency to clean up conditions which generate social unrest. But it has taken a series of riots, a rash of murders, muggings and attacks, and a general demonstration of hostility to make even a part of our comfortable society realize that basic poverty does exist.

## Challenge

. . . Democracy is a word we prize, but it should be more than just a word. . . . A democracy must retain its reason for being . . . a government of the people, by the people, and for the people . . . all the people.

Our nation is now admitting and facing up to its problems of poverty. The real test of the spirit and success of our Great Society will be in what really happens to the 20 per cent of our people who are now destitute . . . and in what attitudes are demonstrated by those who are not.

108 Can a teen-ager do anything to help the destitute?

Robert Lambert in "Underground
Paperbacks" discusses a best-
selling autobiography.


## 67 MANCHILD

Manchild [in the Promised Land] is being read in both ghetto
schools and in the golden suburbs that are around the city. Black
and white, upper-class and lower-class students are finding Claude
Brown's report of his Harlem boyhood intriguing and relevant at a
time when we must understand one another or perish as a democracy.
. . . Perhaps a hundred years from now, people will look back
on books like Manchild and on the slums of Harlem with the same
mixture of outrage and incomprehension with which we now view
the institution of slavery in America. How could men who consider
themselves human impose such conditions on other human beings?
With Claude Brown, we watch his generation of friends and school-
mates being destroyed with the predictable regularity of an infantry
company's casualty rate during the Battle of Verdun. But street
fighting rather than bayonets, jail terms rather than bullets, heroin
rather than shrapnel take the toll of boys and girls. Indeed, the
lives of most of Brown's friends are lived with the fatalism of a
railway timetable. They steal, get caught, go to boy's reformatories, then graduate to jails or penitentiaries. The other possibilities are death through an overdose of heroin or commitment
to an insane asylum for those who have been clubbed too often
or who had been psychically scarred by the brutalizations of poverty.

## Plague of heroin

In the middle of Claude Brown's childhood, the assertion of manhood through fighting diminished as the horrible plague of heroin
swept through Harlem. (One family lost all four sons, dead before
twenty, to the white powder.) The needle replaced the tire chain,
and Harlem became the land of Nodding--that characteristic physical
response to a dose of heroin. Brown himself escaped the scourge
because of a single bad trip sniffing heroin, and because he had no
further need to prove his manhood. But one by one his friends were
found dead from an OD (overdose) or--in the case of girls--pros-
tituting themselves on 125th Street to get money for a fix. One of
the most moving scenes in the book occurs when Brown sees a former
girl friend who has joined the row of needle-punctured girls waiting
to be picked up. Brown pities her enough to buy her a fix, and watches
her administer it, "I watch the syringe as the blood came up into
the drugs that seemed like dirty water. It just filled up with blood,
and as the blood and the drugs started its way down into the needle,
I thought, This is our childhood. Our childhood had been covered
with blood and gone down into somewhere. I wondered where."

## Impossible dream

Not all of Harlem's self-destructiveness and alienation stem
from poverty alone. Parents and children cannot talk to one another.
The older generation, often raised in the rural South where they
couldn't even finish grade school and looked with fear on the fate
of "uppity-niggers," was pathetically unequipped to deal with life
in an industrialized, Northern city. Their aspirations for their
own children remain low. Brown quits his job as a busboy in a
hamburger stand so he can spend more time studying for night
school. His father responds, "Boy, you don't need all that education.
You better keep that job, because that's a good job." Pimp [Claude's
brother] aspires to become an Air Force pilot, but Mama replies:
"'Boy, don't you go wantin' things that ain't for you. You just go
out there and get you a good job.' A good job to Mama was a job
making fifty or sixty dollars a week. . . ." Combined with a low
self-regard, the older Harlem generation maintain an active belief in spiritualism, spells, and voo-doo that further encourages
a fear-drenched fatalism towards life. Pathetically unable to provide models themselves, Brown's parents constantly urge him--or
beat him--so he will "be good," without themselves having any
coherent notion of what "being good" really means.

184

Escape

How, then, did Claude Brown escape the destructiveness of his Harlem boyhood? From a youth of cash register rifling and street brawling, how did he end up as a law student and the author of a best-seller instead of being knifed to death in an alley or sentenced to a twenty-year stretch at Sing-Sing?

First, of course, Claude Brown had battled his way to self-respect while commanding the respect of others: he had no need to prove his manhood through stealing. Second, after an early, youthful robbery he was sent to Wiltwyck--the book is dedicated to "Eleanor Roosevelt, who founded . . . Wiltwyck . . . and to the Wiltwyck School, which is still finding Claude Browns"--where he finally found models of tough humane, compassionate human beings in staff workers like Mr. Papanek--who saw his troubled boys as "people, just plain people"--and Mrs. Cohen--who gave Claude biographies to read which provided further models like Jackie Robinson and Sugar Ray Robinson. Another biography opened up his intellectual life: "I read a book by Albert Schweitzer. He was another fascinating cat. The man knew so much. I really started wanting to know things. I wanted to know things and I wanted to do things."

### Fascinated and repelled

Paradoxically, what allowed Brown to do the things--"I needed to get out of Harlem"--he has done is the very strength that Harlem instilled in him in the first place. For Brown's book is a story of both love and hate towards Harlem. Like Mark Twain in Hannibal, Missouri, a century earlier, Claude Brown is both fascinated by the street--everything happens there in Harlem--and repelled by its casual violence, where Saturday knifings are commonplace. A nostalgia for his youth, and for the earlier, pre-heroin Harlem, pervades the book. "When I was very young . . . I would always be sitting out on the stoop. . . . Even when it was time to go . . . I never wanted to go, because there was so much out there in that street."

### Fatalism

Allied with Brown's need to escape--and ever to return--is a kind of fatalism, a passive acceptance of his life that comes close to being the core theme of the book: for all the horror, each friend found his own way, did his own thing. If they died, they did so with a kind of terrible, twisted integrity. They played to the limit the bad hands dealt them, then folded.

But if there is a calmness, a fatalism, a surprising lack of outrage in Brown's record of his own ascent from hell, this keeps the reader from labeling or rejecting the work as propaganda. It is an intensely human, intensely compassionate work. Perhaps it's for our own good that Brown half-accepts what happened to him. For then it is up to the reader to fully reject those conditions which produce one Claude Brown at the cost of a dozen--or fifty-- brutalized, imprisoned, addicted, or murdered adolescents.

For not everyone can write his way out of Harlem.

109 Contrast the life in your neighborhood with the life that Claude Brown led. What are the differences? The similarities?

Floyd Miller in "The Angel of
Hunter's Point" tells a remarkable
story about an amazing woman.

At 7:30 in the evening of April 9, 1968--the day of Martin
Luther King's funeral--bus No. 42 was just completing its regular run from the heart of San Francisco to Hunters Point, a ghetto
neighborhood near Candlestick Park. At Evans Avenue near Grif-
fith Street, four Negro teen-age boys crowded aboard. Within
seconds there was the sound of a single shot, and the boys, their
hands full of money, came tumbling out of the bus and disappeared
into the warren of darkening streets. The white driver, Martin
Whitted, was dead.

Minutes later a police car arrived, then another and another.
Moments before the murder there had been sniper fire from the
surrounding hills, and now the police crouched behind their
battered vehicles, prepared for the worst.

San Francisco was not the only city with racial troubles that
emotion-charged night, and it was not until some time later that
I became aware of the events in Hunters Point. I was first alerted
by an article I read in Christian Century. It read, in part:

Concomitant with the acts of violence that followed in the wake
of the assassination of Martin Luther King, Jr., were some
exemplary acts of compassion. In San Francisco, a young
white mother's reaction to the murder of her husband by
Negro youths was so extraordinary, so moving, so loving--

in the deepest sense--that it served to assuage and transform a tense and volatile situation.

On April 16, the San Francisco Chronicle ran an editorial that said, "Mrs. Dixie Whitted's proposal that a memorial fund in her husband's name be established to benefit young people of the Hunters Point area is an act of grace, an act of compassion, an act of hope for the city."

San Francisco's Mayor Joseph Alioto was quoted as saying, "She must be one of the city's most remarkable women."

I took a plane to San Francisco to see for myself.

## Rare women

The Whitteds had been active members of St. Mark's Lutheran Church. I went to the old brick structure at 1111 O'Farrell Street to talk with the Reverend Ross Hidy, a large, well-proportioned man with a square, handsome face and a touch of gray at the temples.

"Can you explain Dixie Whitted?" I asked. "What is she like?"

"I'll try. She came here from Washington State some years ago, worked in a bank until she met a young marine named Martin Whitted and married him. They have three enchanting little girls. She is 29 years old."

He paused thoughtfully. "Dixie is a simple woman, simple in the way saints are simple--possessed of a rare gift for doing what is right. The Hunters Point project was her idea; every statement she made was her own. That's how she was able to touch the heart of this great but sometimes cynical city. And for all her sweet gentleness, there is steel in her. You'll see what I mean when you talk to her."

## Pretty and shy

The Whitted apartment was in the Mission district of San Francisco, a neighborhood of deteriorating flats but clean streets. At the top of a gloomy flight of stairs Dixie Whitted awaited me with her daughters--three-year-old Erica, five-year-old Kelly and Robin, who looked about nine. Dixie shyly extended her hand and announced that there was coffee on the stove. We sat at the kitchen table to drink it while the children studied me from various angles, finally lost interest and drifted away.

Dixie Whitted was smaller and prettier and shyer than I had

expected. It was difficult to imagine her playing a public role in a race crisis. "Dixie," I said, "your husband made the run into Hunters Point many times. Did it worry you?"

She shook her head. "He knew the people there. He liked them and they liked him. He received letters every now and then, fan letters, sort of. Last month he got a poem."

From the jumbled interior of her purse she retrieved a piece of ruled notebook paper that had been folded and unfolded many times. The penciled words on it were already fading. It read:

Wish they were all as nice as you
Calling out transfer points--answering questions too.
And since you do it with a smile
That's what makes it worthwhile.

However it might rate as poetry, it was a moving tribute to a man.

"Dixie, where were you when you heard about Martin?"

Her eyes seemed to focus on something far away. She said softly, "I was here. I was reading a bedtime story to the children --"Jack and the Beanstalk." I'll never again be able to read that story."

For a long moment she swirled the cold, forgotten coffee in the thick cup. "The next morning I told the children. Robin is old enough to understand all about what happened. Erica is so young she doesn't understand any of it. But for Kelly it's terribly difficult because she can understand only a part. She knows her daddy has gone away, but she believes he will come back to her."

Tense moments

That morning of April 10, while Dixie was telling her children that their father was dead, the city was tense and sullen. The trouble at Hunters Point had been brief, put down by massive police response. Now there was evidence that plans were being made by both sides. On street corners men stood together to speak in low tones--white men in some of the white neighborhoods, black men in some of the black neighborhoods. San Francisco seemed headed toward a widening racial chasm across which no meaningful words could be spoken, none heard.

But then a voice did speak, and it was heard. The young widow said simply that her husband had been killed, not because of his color, but for robbery. The murderers would have done the same

190

thing to anybody, black or white, she declared.

When her statement appeared in the newspapers, the city seemed to pause in its drift toward the brink. There was a breathing spell, a precious moment to consider. Offers of help began to arrive at Dixie's apartment--jobs, food, cash.

"There was more than I could use," she explained to me. "And it seemed--well, sinful that I should benefit by Martin's death. It seemed to me that the kids at Hunters Point needed help more than I did."

### TV plea

It was then that she conceived the idea of a Martin Whitted Memorial Fund. She talked it over with Pastor Hidy, who made the announcement to the press and personally took a copy to a TV station. The news director asked Hidy if he could persuade Dixie to repeat her proposal on television.

"I think she would do it if she was convinced it would be helpful," Hidy said.

"At first I didn't want to do it," Dixie told me. "I was scared I might break down. But then I remembered how Mrs. Martin Luther King had behaved during her husband's funeral. I wanted to act as well as she had acted."

When Dixie appeared before the cameras the impact on the viewers was considerable. San Francisco saw a pretty and composed young woman who spoke softly, almost in a whisper, but with words that went to the heart of the problem that afflicted them all. She asked for contributions to the Martin Whitted Memorial Fund, to be administered by the city's Human Rights Commission. Her only proviso was that the young of Hunters Point were to decide how the money was spent. Only once, when she spoke of her husband's love for his children, did her eyes fill with tears. But she blinked rapidly and they did not spill over.

### Response

"What was the response from the TV audience?" I asked.

Her face lighted up with pride. "Martin's fund is now over $9000. I've received hundreds of letters." She pointed to two large cardboard cartons filled with letters from well-wishers --one even from a prisoner in a state penitentiary.

The Memorial service for Martin Whitted was held at St.

Mark's on Monday morning, April 15. All the municipal buses
ran with headlights on, and many private cars rolled to work
with black crepe or ribbon tied to radio antennas. The church
was filled to overflowing a half hour before the service. Mayor
Alioto led the contingent from city hall. Labor officials attended,
as did religious leaders, cultural leaders, and bus drivers,
black and white.

The widow was escorted into the church and the memorial
service, jointly conducted by a Negro and a white minister,
began. Pastor Hidy spoke of the two Martins, one a Negro who
was "perhaps a saint," the other white and a "good man." He
observed that the nation could ill afford to lose either of them.
Of the widow he said, "We shall never know just what influence
the words of Dixie Whitted had in the minds of people in the Bay
Area. But it well might be that our city owes to this quiet and
soft-spoken saint of God a debt that might defy description."

At the end of the service the coffin was carried out of the
church by six pallbearers, most of them Martin's friends
and associates. Three were white men, and three were black.

## Simplicity and love

I asked Dixie Whitted if I might look through the family picture album. On the very first page was a picture of Dixie's and
Martin's wedding party, standing in front of St. Mark's. There
were two couples in attendance--one of them black.

"That's Given Llewelly and her husband," she explained. "I
met her at the bank where I got my first job in San Francisco."

"Why did you have them at your wedding?" I asked.

She seemed surprised. "Why, she's one of my best friends."

"Did you and your husband see them socially?"

"Yes," she said, still puzzled at the direction of my questions.

"Dixie, do you belong to any interracial organizations?"

"No." There was a slight note of apology in her voice. "I just
stay home and take care of my babies."

"Do you and Given talk together about the race problem?"

"No, not much." She frowned in concentration. "Maybe it's
because we know each other so well on the inside that we forget
what we look like on the outside."

I thought I understood Dixie Whitted at last. Her strength came
from her indomitable innocence, the kind of innocence that rises
from simplicity and love, that rejects prejudice as too alien to be
understood.

Unnoticed by either of us, five-year-old Kelly had come into the kitchen and was looking at the family snapshots. "That's my daddy!" she squealed, pointing to a picture of Martin posing on a beach as a strong man--his three daughters clinging to his arms.

With a suddenly troubled face she turned to her mother and said, "I'm worried about my daddy." Then she burst into tears.

Dixie pulled her daughter hard against her. Gently rocking back and forth, she sang a tuneless phrase deep in her throat. "There there . . . baby . . . there there."

I left as soon as I decently could.

### New hope

That evening, while going over my interview notes, I discovered that I had carried away one of Dixie's letters--the one from the prisoner. He identified himself as a Negro, and wrote: "I owe you a debt. You've never known me but in your way, by your deep understanding, the beauty of your refusal to hate, you have increased my potential for humanism. I'll never again be able to hate collectively all white men. What a monument you and your children are to your husband's memory."

I recalled a phrase Dixie had spoken during our day together: "Martin would have wanted some good to come from his death."

It has.

110 What struck you most in this account of Dixie Whitted? What makes some people respond to evil and hate with love and others not?

Joy Marie Hoag in "The Mounting
Problem of Teen-Age Shoplifting"
explores a growing community
problem.

## 69 THE STEALER

Shoplifters in stores across the nation have added more than
half a billion dollars to our cost of living this year. . . . The
typical shoplifter today is a teen-ager from a good family!
    . . . Out of 6500 confessed shoplifters last year in Alexander's
New York stores, 3500 were teen-agers, most of them girls.
. . . In Detroit, the Women's Division of the Police Department
reports that among female shoplifters, 14-year-olds outnumber
all other ages. IBM records of shoplifting cases at Shillito's, a
leading Cincinnati department store, show that 78 out of every
100 shoplifters are under 18. A recent Gilbert Youth Research
survey of 1,281 young people across the nation revealed that
more than half knew other teens who were regular shoplifters.

Strange

Most of these offenders are not from families of a low income
bracket. And they're not stealing necessities, but luxuries
they could pay for with the spending money in their pockets.
Here are some cases that recently gained public attention:
    Seven star basketball players at Riggs high school in Pierre,
S.D., were expelled for shoplifting. They'd been adding ex-
citement to their out-of-town game trips by heisting items
in the sweater-to-necktie-clip range from local stores. Not one

of the boys came from an underprivileged family.

In a town in Washington, police broke up a shoplifting ring of 25 high school girls who within the past year had stolen up to $4000 worth of clothing and accessories. The juvenile bureau officer assigned to the case said that most admitted they didn't need the stolen goods and most were nice-looking, well-mannered girls from middle-class families, girls who'd never been in trouble before even with school authorities. . . .

## What to do?

This phenomenon of shoplifting by "privileged" children has been increasing at a rapid rate since the Second World War, but getting a true picture has been difficult because so many of the offenses never become statistical. Timid and overly-cautious merchants have avoided notifying police or newspapers, preferring to just call the parents and ask for return of the stolen articles or reimbursement. Enough high pressure from prominent parents has even discouraged this defense. In Chappaqua, storeowners who tried talking to the mothers and fathers of youths caught in the act got such indignant denials, accusations and bullying threats of boycotts that they soon gave it up and began chalking up the shortages to normal business expense.

In another community one retailer went to visit the parents of a teen-ager who'd admitted swiping 18 sweaters and 17 skirts from his store and others over a period of several weeks. "The mother screamed at me, seemed to think it was all my fault," the bewildered man said later.

## Too tempting

. . . One of the most obvious causes, of course, is a revolution in merchandising that has made it much easier to shoplift. Many department, variety, drug and grocery stores have been turned into self-service stores with only a minimum of sales personnel. Items that were once in showcases or shelves behind counters are now openly displayed within easy access of the light-fingered "shopper." And new tempting methods of setting out goods so as to lure impulse buyers are proving to make the goods just as irresistible to young shoplifters.

. . . Faced with such losses, more and more merchants are no longer soft-pedaling shoplifting and have abandoned their traditional scold-them-and-send-them-home policy. Instead they're adopting such aggressive tactics as teen-age security patrols; radio equipment for detectives who dress and act like customers; TV cameras for spotting offenders; elaborate systems of mirrors in plain view so that customers are aware of being watched ("An ounce of prevention is worth a pound of apprehension"); larger and more bulky packaging making it more difficult to secret items away in pockets or purses; and central file indexes on all apprehended shoplifters.

## Deeper problem

. . . Some people contend that these preventive, on-the-surface measures can have only limited effects, that the basic cause of the problem is a lowering of moral standards. Storekeepers and detectives alike testify to a brazen, cynical attitude on the part of many apprehended youths, a complete lack of remorse. One retailer in an affluent suburb could recall only one youngster, out of hundreds he'd caught shoplifting, who showed any guilt feelings.

## Not stealing?

Department store managers in another high-income community reported that most young offenders gave answers such as: "You can afford it," "Everybody in my gang does it," "My parents are good customers of yours," "It's not really like stealing."
. . . Many of the youngsters guilty of shoplifting seem to see it as a romantic, exciting pastime rather than as a moral issue. "It was just a way of getting kicks," one 17-year-old told a judge.
. . . "It was sort of secret, scary fun," admitted one high-school sophomore. The secrecy, the feeling of "putting it over" on the adults, seems to be a definite part of the appeal, so parents and merchants who try to cover up the behavior may be perpetuating it.
On the other hand, bringing the situation out in the open seems to curtail it. One courageous PTA group decided to publicize a committee report on extensive juvenile shoplifting in its upper class community. Parents, faculty and school administrators discussed it openly, frankly calling the offense "stealing." Teachers were surprised to notice in the classrooms a general air of relief that the matter had finally come out into the open. The aura of secret adventure that had surrounded shoplifting suddenly seemed to fade, and shrinkage in the local stores shrunk.

111 Why do you think bringing
shoplifting out in the open and
calling it "stealing" has helped?

Shoplifting clubs

. . . High school shoplifting clubs have been uncovered in many
communities like Oklahoma City where the girls began by pilfering
school supplies and "graduated" to downtown stores. Some groups
even specify the lifting of $25 worth of merchandise or specific
articles like cashmere sweaters by potential members.

To resist such pressures requires a certain kind of heroism
that few adults understand. The urge to conform, to belong, to
avoid the label of "chicken" is a powerful one in the adolescent's
heart. A 15-year-old newcomer to her community and school
explained the reasons for her shoplifting bout to a juvenile court
officer this way: "Everybody was stealing stuff. We all knew it.
They laughed at you if you paid."

This is no blanket indictment of our country's young people.
Juvenile shoplifters are a minority, fortunately, but the recent
increase in their ranks is enough to warrant some serious soul-
searching.

112  How prevalent is dishonesty
(stealing, cheating, etc.) among
young people you personally
know?

Albert Lesco in "My Prison World
Is Too Small!" reflects upon a
life that he would like to forget.

## 70 THE LONER

Perhaps a good place to begin my story is with an incident that
took place one day when I was a student in junior high. The school
principal had called me in for counseling, and had lectured me
at some length--about my low grades, habitual tardiness, and
a few instances of truancy. He went on to complain about my poor
attitude in general, and also my choice of friends.

Now I considered this principal to be extremely naive and
something of a prude. A self-righteous square, I thought, so in-
hibited by puritanical concepts that there could not possibly be
any real understanding between us. I really didn't see why he
had to make a federal case out of these trivial matters. Sure,
I deserved some punishment--a few hours of after-school de-
tention maybe--so why didn't he just tell me what it was going
to be and get off my back! But he seemed to have something else
on his mind.

Corny

"Young man," he finally said, "if you don't change your ways
--and your choice of associates--one of these days you are going
to find yourself in more trouble than you can handle." He paused,
I recall, and appeared to be studying me closely. Then, in an
ominous tone and with carefully measured words, he added, "You
may even find yourself in some penitentiary."

199 / social unconcern

Well, now that was getting a little far out, I thought, and of course I was not about to be impressed by his corny dramatics. . . .

The principal's mention of prison did shake me up a bit though. But only because it made me wonder just how much he knew, or suspected, concerning some of the things my buddies and I had been mixed up in. He hadn't mentioned any of these things, but I was thinking about some recent acts of vandalism, some petty shoplifting, and once when we had borrowed an automobile without the owner's consent.

The above paragraphs were written by Albert Lesco, who is currently serving a 25-year prison sentence in the Kansas State Penitentiary in Lansing, Kansas. They appeared in an article he recently wrote. Later on in the article Lesco makes these candid observations.

## Looking back

. . . Today that little scene from the past has come to occupy a big place in my thoughts about myself. I've learned that those behavior and attitude patterns, observed by the school principal such a long time ago, were even then shaping the course of my life. . . .

It may be impossible for anyone to precisely pinpoint the time when my world began to shrink. Looking back, however, I can see some landmarks. These were signs . . .

One of these signs was the habit of deception, which I began to develop at an early age. Habit is the right word for it, because deceiving people became an almost compulsive thing with me. . . . I was also deceiving myself. The puzzling thing, now that I have thought about it, is that there never was any real reason for all this deception. At least not at first. Oh, perhaps I sometimes lied to get attention from someone--or maybe to get revenge. I don't really know. But telling falsehoods got to be such a habit that I am quite sure I often did it for no reason at all, except just for the sake of lying.

## Rattle game

There were more subtle forms of deception too. Like the times I sneaked money out of the small coin bank I had. And every time I removed a coin from the bank, I'd replace it with a metal washer (swiped from my grandfather's workshop). That was so I could rattle the bank's contents and no one would realize the coins were missing. When relatives would visit our home, I'd get my little bank out and rattle it for them. Almost invariably they would give me a coin or two to add to my "savings," which I would promptly replace with more washers as soon as I was out of their sight.

When I was no longer satisfied with just the few coins obtained in this manner, I then started swiping small sums from other sources--from a purse someone carelessly left laying some-where, . . . and even from my dad's trousers while he was tak-ing a nap.

## Loneliness

Eventually I began to experience deep feelings of guilt about all the lying, cheating, and petty stealing I had been doing. These activities had forced a secrecy upon me that made me feel lonely and strange. Keeping secrets with yourself can become a very large burden, I discovered. It makes you feel isolated from others. . . . there is no lonelier man in the world than a man who is alone with his guilt.

. . . It was not until I had served time in three penitentiaries that I gave any serious thought to going straight. Then I tried it, and liked it--for awhile. But the habit of dishonesty had too strong a hold on me it seemed. I felt it necessary to deceive people about my past life--to lie about what I had done and where I had been. On the surface my life was respectable and satisfying. But be-hind the facade of apparent respectability I was experiencing the misery of my concealed guilt, made increasingly unbearable each day by my fear of exposure and disgrace. Again, as in my youth, I felt isolated from society. Only this time it was worse. Eventually I turned once more to crime, convinced in my own mind that it was inevitable--that there was no other way for me to go.

Back in prison, . . . I am able to see my world as it really is. . . . My guilt feelings are not now the disturbing problem they once were, because my guilt is no longer a hidden thing.

But the shame of my past will always be with me, and the record of my past will stand.

113 How did Lesco's habit of deception: 1) start, 2) lead to loneliness?

A junior thinks about breaking
the rules--and one's self.


## 71 GOT IT LICKED!

My buddy was bragging at the lunch table. "And when the old
man at the cash register turned his back, I slipped the sweater
under my coat. A $14.95 sweater! Guys, I've got this game licked."

It's easy to beat the odds, to break the rules: run a stop sign,
cheat in an exam, palm a pen! But who's kidding whom? What good
does it do us to swipe five bucks or ditch Mass for a few months?
Actually, laws are made for our own good. By breaking them, we
only hurt ourselves--and other people.

God, you gave me the free will to do as I wish. Give me the
grace to think before I act. Help me to see that I never gain by
breaking the rules.

"The law . . . is to me more precious than thousands of gold
and silver pieces." Psalm 118:72.

114 How do most people regard
Christ's commandments: 1) as
restrictions to freedom, 2) as guides
to happiness, 3) as opportunities to
follow Christ? What is the difference between the three?

## 72 BAD NIGHT

A sophomore describes another
common neighborhood problem.

We were sitting in the Tastee Freeze parking lot in a car owned
by my buddy's parents--who also own the Tastee Freeze. It was
kind of cold, so we had the motor running and the heat on. We
also had the radio playing. The headlights were on, and so were
the emergency blinkers.

A police car rode by about 9:20. One of the guys said he saw
the cops pointing in our direction. (The car went by rather slow.)
We didn't think anything more about it, because this goes on a lot
in my neighborhood. All four of us were smoking, and we were
having a good bull session. (Two of the guys were back from
boarding school for the weekend.)

About ten minutes later, we heard a siren. The same cop car
rolled up with the siren and the flasher going full blast. As they
pulled into the parking lot, they blocked the entrance by putting
the car sideways across the exit.

The cops jumped out of the car quickly with their billy clubs
out and the holster guards unsnapped. They shouted, "Get out
of the car, you punks!"

They lined us up and started to search the first guy. (I think
I ought to make it known that all of us have been picked up by
the cops before; the exact same incident occurred at the same
place two months earlier.)

While one cop searched the first guy, the second one ordered

204

the hood and trunk opened. He checked the carburetor, took off the fan belt, messed up the trunk, and made himself obnoxious. He said he thought some of the parts were stolen and that the car was stolen, too. Unfortunately, we didn't have any papers in the car. But luckily the owner of the Tastee Freeze pulled up. (She was one of the kid's mother.) The cops shut up fast, and said it was just routine. Less than ten seconds later, they drove off. They created quite an incident, wasted about an hour, and we couldn't do a thing about it, because they didn't accuse us of anything.

### Another incident

I went bowling with three of my friends on the first Thursday after Christmas. We finished bowling and were walking out at 10:26. I stopped to buy a coke from a machine. My three friends didn't bother to wait. They were already out of the door by the time I got my coke. I walked out of the door at 10:28. I know because I checked my watch.

A squad car pulled up to my three friends and told them to get in. The cops didn't see me, so I cut back into the bowling alley.

The next day I found out that one of the guys got a curfew violation. (There were two 17-year-olds and one 15-year-old.) The guy that got it--he was 15--lives about a half a block from the bowling alley. He could have made it home in thirty seconds. Can you blame teen-agers for losing respect for authority?

115  Has anything similar to this happened to you? How should a person respond to what he thinks is unfairness?

### Hard-nosed?

By way of contrast, a Peoria high-school student had this to say about police.

And what about our policemen? There is a thankless job if I ever saw one. The police are fine when they save your life or property. But let them show up when you want to risk someone else's life by doing 60 in a 30 mile zone and they are your worst enemy.

I know a kid who was stopped for speeding. The cop was a

nice guy and let him off with a warning. Do you think this kid was grateful? Not him! He spent the next week bragging about how he faked the fuzz. Is it any wonder why so many police officers become so hard nosed?

116 What is the attitude of most teen-agers toward police?

## 73 TEN O'CLOCK TELECAST

A junior reflects on a proper
attitude toward certain adults.

Late reports indicate that last night's rioting caused an esti-
mated one million dollars in damage. Fighting continues in the
Near East. Dope peddlers arrested in high-school parking lot.

The world is in a big mess. Many people, particularly the
young, are looking for some guide to life. But too often the adults,
those who could give youth the greatest amount of aid and guidance,
are found wanting. Young people seek and expect much help from
their elders, but we are often disillusioned by their conduct.

Lord, help the older generation to understand and to help the
younger one.

Then Jesus spoke to the crowds and to his disciples. "The
teachers of the Law and the Pharisees," he said, "are the authorized interpreters of Moses' Law. So you must obey and follow
everything they tell you to do; do not, however, imitate their actions, because they do not practice what they preach." Matthew 23:1-3.

117 How does the gospel passage
at the end of this reflection hold
true for many young people today?

Within my earthly temple, there's a crowd;
There's one of us that's humble, and one that's proud;
There's one that's broken-hearted for his sins
And one who unrepentant sits and grins.
There's one who loves his neighbor as himself;
And one who cares for naught but fame and self.
From much corroding care I should be free,
If once I could decide which one is me.  Anonymous

208

# CHAPTER 5

# SCHOOL WORLD

> I don't know, but I think I'm go-
> ing through a phase or something.

## 74 "QUICK JOEY SMALL"

I just heard a record on the radio called, "Quick Joey Small."
The more often I hear it, the more it seems to fit my life. The
first line is, "Quick Joey Small went over the wall."

This is what I feel like doing. I have a great urge to get away
from it all--forget about school and home and just leave. You
might call it the sophomore "slump."

The song, later, goes on to tell how the sheriff was chasing
him. The one line, "Sheriff has a shotgun; he'll fill you full of
lead, son," describes the do-or-die of my life. Either go to
school, or drop out and not get a good job.

Or the line, "Deputy has a blackjack; he'll blast your head with
one whack," describes all the disciplinary measures that can be
taken against me if I "break out."

Getting worse

I don't know if you remember, but in one of my earlier papers
I said I adopted a "don't give a damn policy." Well, it seems to
be getting worse. I just got two pink slips (danger of flunking),
one in math and one in Latin. The only reason I got them was
lack of effort on my part. One of the reasons I came to this
school was that I was good in math. Granted, I am having a lot
of trouble in one part of my math, but I often find myself

making simple, stupid mistakes. I thought I was doing pretty well in Latin, but again I found myself making simple, stupid mistakes. I found that I just lost complete interest in homework and studies. I found I was daydreaming more and wishing I was out with the guys. In the past month I have a sudden wish to get a job. I don't know if I'm going through a phase or something.

I just can't seem to wait for the weekends. When I'm free, I feel almost like a blind man seeing for the first time. I'm very happy when I'm out with the guys, but when school starts, I find myself again waiting for the weekends.

My schoolwork is off and even when I'm with the guys they are beginning to think of me as a loner. The last time we went out together, all I heard was, "What the hell is the matter with you, Pollack, you in love or somethin'?"

118  Have you ever felt this way? If you were this boy's student counselor, how would you try to help him?

## 75 THE REAL ME?

Do people ever see the real me?
If not, whose fault is it?

Harold Blake Walker tells how Nathaniel Hawthorne left among
his papers the outline to a play that he never got a chance to write.
The play centers around a man who never appears on stage. All
kinds of secondary characters make their entry and exit during
the play, but the principal character never appears.

In a sense, Hawthorne's play would have been a play about
every man. God intended the real you and the real me to be the
principal character in the plays Your Life and My Life. Oddly
enough, however, the real you and the real me rarely step out
on stage. Instead, all kinds of secondary selves appear. The
sinner in me, the coward, the weakling--all of these secondary
selves steal the show from our real selves. These secondary
selves march out onto the stage while our real selves remain in
the wings.

119 Why do our secondary
selves frequently steal the
spotlight from our real
selves?

Most of us are not one person but three persons: the one we
think we are, the one other people think we are, and the person
that we actually are.

We are two people: one good
guy and one bad guy.

The Strange Case of Dr. Jekyll and Mr. Hyde was written by
Robert Louis Stevenson (1850-1894). The story deals with a person who induces a split personality. By taking a drug, Dr. Jekyll
is able to take on a repulsive, dwarfish body. In this form, he
operates as Mr. Edward Hyde and indulges in his evil drives. A
renewal of the drug allows him to reassume his taller form and
become again the kind of doctor that he is. Failure to get the drug
in time leads to trouble.

The story of Dr. Jekyll and Mr. Hyde made such an impact
upon the public that Jekyll and Hyde have become symbols of the
good and bad in human nature.

Stevenson got the idea for the story from his recollections of a
notorious person of his time who was a respected craftsman by
day and a burglar by night. The story took shape in Stevenson's
mind while he was recovering from a fever. He wrote the first
draft, about 30,000 words (one hundred typewritten, double-spaced
pages) in three days. Dissatisfied with it, he burned this version
and completed the present version in another three days. (How
many people today take such pride in their work?) The book sold
40,000 copies in six months. (Quite a feat in a day when book-
stores were not so available.) The novel has since become a
classic and was made into a movie--shown on TV.

All of us, to some extent, are Dr. Jekylls and Mr. Hydes. We are two people wrapped in one skin. One of us is pretty good; the other is not so good.

When things are going our way, we are usually good and fun to be with. We are all smiles and pleasant to everyone. As long as things keep going our way, we are walking saints. We never talk back to our parents; we never cut the other guy down; we never blow up at our brothers and sisters. After a while we can get the idea that we are fine young Christians.

## Turnabout

Then comes the revelation. Someone cuts us short. Or some-one crosses us up--or upsets our plans for the day or the week-end. We don't get our way. Suddenly the good guy in us goes into hiding, and the bad guy in us comes roaring out.

An old Uncle Remus story illustrates how quickly this can take place. The story concerns a rabbit, a fox, and a tar baby.

Brer Rabbit, you will recall, imagined himself to be a pretty clever guy. He had outwitted Brer Fox at every turn. Brer Fox was unhappy about all of this and decided to get even with Brer Rabbit. He made a lifelike statue out of tar and turpentine. He named his creation Tar Baby.

One day he placed Tar Baby in the middle of the road and scampered off into the bushes to await the arrival of Brer Rabbit.

Brer Fox didn't have long to wait. Shortly Brer Rabbit came cruising down the road. When he spotted Tar Baby, he screeched to a halt. Then remembering his manners, he bade the stranger a good day, and he inquired how Tar Baby felt this bright morn-ing. Tar Baby made no response. Offended, Brer Rabbit lost his composure. He was too important to be ignored. Finally, Brer Rabbit lost his temper and belted Tar Baby on the side of the head. His hand stuck. Tar Baby still said nothing. Next, Brer Rabbit slugged Tar Baby with his other hand, and got it stuck too. Then Brer Rabbit lost the use of both of his feet, as he tried kicking Tar Baby. Finally, he got his head stuck when he butted Tar Baby.

At this point Brer Fox leaped from the bushes and rolled on the ground in hysterical laughter. Uncle Remus ended the story without saying whether or not Brer Fox ate Brer Rabbit. But we can draw our own conclusions.

A mirror

The story of Brer Rabbit is, to some extent, the story of all of us. It is a kind of mirror into which we can look and see ourselves as we really are. We are two people: one good guy and one bad guy. We are good guys as long as things go our way and people treat us the way we think they ought to treat us. But when they don't, the bad guy in us suddenly pops out. What is this?

120 Is man basically good? Basically bad? Neither? Explain your answer.

"I find that I have the will to
do good, but not the power."

## 77 THE KEY

Each one of us is the victim of what is
called original sin. Among other things,
this expression means that within all of
us there goes on a constant tug-of-war
between good and evil. St. Paul referred
to it when he said:

I often find that I have the will to do
good, but not the power. That is, I
don't accomplish the good I set out to
do, and the evil I don't really want to
do I find I am always doing. Romans 7:19.

St. Paul goes on to say, "who on earth
can set me free from the clutches of my own
sinful nature? I thank God there is a way
out through Jesus Christ our Lord."

Christ was a man just as human as you
and I. Unfortunately, we tend to forget this.
We think of him only as God who could do
anything. We look upon him as having it
made in every way.

Nothing could be more wrong than this

oversimplified view of Christ. Just as Christ was true God, he was also true man. This means that he had all the human drives and emotions that we have. When he was unjustly accused, tortured, and put to death, he felt the same hot surge of human anger that we would have felt. Instead of blowing up or turning into a hate-filled person, however, he remained himself. He was always in control, even when the whole tide of events turned against him.

## Power

Christ won his victory over evil. He also wants us to win our victory over evil. He offers to each of us the power we need to fight successfully against the enemy within us.

Mobilizing the power of Christ is not simply a matter of saying a few magic words or pushing some magic button. On the contrary, it requires constant courageous effort. It means that we must constantly: 1) reflect on the inspiration of Christ's life in our prayer, and 2) seek out the power of Christ's life in the Mass and sacraments.

## Stick at it

We will undoubtedly be tempted to throw in the towel many times as we seek to win the tug-of-war between good and evil within us. But Christ promises us that if we keep struggling and remain united to him, we will emerge victorious. Christ said:

> You must go on growing in me and I will grow in you. For just as a branch cannot bear any fruit unless it shares the life of the vine, so you can produce nothing unless you go on growing in me. . . . For the plain fact is that apart from me you can do nothing at all. John 15:4-6.

121 Why are we so prone to think of Christ only as God? What episodes in the Gospel show his human side in a special way?

216

## 78 WATER WALKER

> "He's no failure. He's not
> dead yet." W. L. George.

Defeat and discouragement bug all of us at times. Someone
has called them the secret arsenal of Satan. When a man gets
discouraged, he becomes the prey to all kinds of difficulties.
He gets down on life and himself. He becomes gruff and short-
tempered around his friends. He makes life miserable for everyone. He loses his perspective and balance.

What about discouragement and defeat? Can they serve any
useful purpose in our life? Or are they things that we just have
to learn to put up with?

The answer to this question depends on each one of us individually.
Psychologists tell us that discouragement can make us either bitter
or better. It is entirely up to us to decide which it will be. We can
either give up or get up. We have within ourselves the power to
turn discouragement into either a cross or a blessing. How so?
An example may help.

Doctors tell us that when a person comes face to face with a
deadly enemy, adrenalin pours into his system. He feels a burst
of energy that prepares him for either fight or flight.

Discouragement can act in a similar way. A stunning setback
--being cut from a school play cast or team, failing a big test--
jolts us. It suddenly brings us face to face with ourselves. We
are suddenly forced to take stock of ourselves and to make a
decision about our way of doing things. Perhaps we have been

living in a dream world. The shock of defeat or discouragement can suddenly awaken us. Perhaps we have been trying to go it alone--without Christ. The shock of defeat or discouragement can remind us that trying to live without Christ is like trying to keep alive without food.

Defeat can act as a kind of spiritual adrenalin. Once the initial shock is over, it can trigger our energy. It can force us to concentrate our efforts in a way we would not have done had we not experienced defeat or discouragement. It can help us tap new powers and resources that we never dreamed existed in us.

### Turning point

In the opinion of nearly all of his biographers, the turning point in the life of Franklin Roosevelt, the only man to be elected president three times, was the attack of polio that struck him down as a young man. Life magazine called it the "real educative process of his life." Speaking of the effect of this apparent tragedy, Frances Perkins says in her book, The Roosevelt I Knew, "The man emerged completely warmhearted, with humility of spirit and with a deeper philosophy."

### Progress point

God speaks to us in time of discouragement. He tells us that it is merely a time of testing and trial. Defeat and discouragement are not intended to be stumbling blocks, hindering our progress. Rather they are to be stepping-stones, which make true progress possible. It is up to us to take advantage of them. Here is how God himself speaks about them.

When all kinds of trials and temptations crowd into your lives . . . don't resent them as intruders, but welcome them as friends! Realize that they come to test your faith and to produce in you the quality of endurance. But let the process go on until you become men of mature character with the right sort of independence. And if, in the process, any of you does not know how to meet any particular problem he has only to ask God-- who gives generously to all men without making them feel foolish or guilty--and he may be quite sure that the necessary wisdom will be given him. But he must ask in sincere faith without secret doubts as to whether he really wants God's help or not. The man who trusts God, but with inward reservations, is like a wave of

218

the sea, carried forward by the wind one moment and driven
back the next. That sort of man cannot hope to receive anything from the Lord. . . . The man who patiently endures the
temptations and trials that come to him is the truly happy
man. James 1:2-8,12.

> 122  What methods do you use
> to overcome discouragement
> when it hits?

Water walking

The battle against discouragement and defeat will continue
throughout life. In some battles we will experience success; in
other battles, failure. But the only true defeat is to give up. The
only true defeat is to forget about Christ and to leave him out of
the picture. Christ is the key figure in our battle against discouragement. If we put our confidence and trust in him, we will be
unbeatable--no matter how many times we fall.

Putting all of your trust in Christ is not easy. It takes courage,
but above all, it takes great faith. It is a lot like walking on water.
Some people say that it can't be done. They say that it is impossible. When we are tempted to agree with them, we should reread
and reflect on the meaning of the gospel episode narrated in
Matthew 14:22-23.

> 123  Read the gospel episode.
> How is each one of us like Peter?
> What lesson does Christ wish to
> teach us in this episode?

## 79 REEL OR REAL

A high-school student reflects
on life and its darker moments.

Everyone has his bad days. An executive groans, "I sure don't
feel like getting up today. Jim can fill in for me. I think I'll call in
sick." A student moans, "Another history test--fifty questions!
Who does that teacher think he is asking us to work like that every
night? I feel like throwing my book out the window--or at him."

We all feel like quitting at times. We constantly look for the
easy way out. In the reel world of films and TV, wonderful things
happen to people. But in the real world of life, success comes
only with hard work and suffering.

Lord, help us to accept ourselves and our situations. Help us
to make our minds the masters of our bodies. Give us the courage
and maturity to face up to life's challenges.

"The sufferings of the present time are not worthy to be compared with the glory to come." Romans 8:18.

124 Do movies and TV paint an
unrealistic view of life and success? Be concrete and give
examples to back up your opinion.

> Instead of helping us, defeat and
> discouragement can hinder us.

Instead of making you better, the problems you now face can make you bitter. Instead of becoming stepping-stones to maturity and adulthood, your problems can become stumbling blocks to progress.

Defeat and discouragement can give us a negative outlook on life. They can give us what psychologists call the no-complex. A person with a no-complex is one who habitually takes a dim view of everything. For example, if someone gets a new idea, the man with a no-complex will immediately tend to say, "It won't work."

The dictionary defines the negativist (a man with a no-complex) as one whose attitude is marked by skepticism. He naturally tends to throw cold water on new ideas.

Block to progress

It has been said that the person with the no-complex has done more to block human and scientific progress than any other person. Author John Kent in "Watch Out for the Negativist" says:

Almost every inventor and innovator can document the opposition to his ideas from the "experts" and from those in authority. The genius who first devised the wheel was no doubt met with a jeering "It won't work." Human nature has not changed since then.

Consider, for example, the opposition that was encountered by Samuel F. B. Morse when he proposed sending electrical pulses over wire to carry a message. Congress called the idea absurd. But Morse persisted and built a 38-mile telegraph line from Washington, D.C. to Baltimore. On May 24th, 1844, when the historic message "What hath God wrought!" was flashed over the line, Congress admitted that the idea worked.

## He laughed

When young George Westinghouse presented his ideas about a new type of train brake to Commodore Cornelius Vanderbilt, the powerful railroad magnate laughed and dismissed him with: "If I understand you, young man, you propose to stop a railroad train with wind. I have no time to listen to such nonsense!" But within a few years other railroads were replacing their hand brakes with air brakes, and Westinghouse was on his way to becoming a major U.S. industrialist.

## Chopper incident

Kent goes on to point out that the negativist tends to take a dim view of new things even when he must admit that they are workable. Kent cites the example of the modern helicopter. In the early 1940's leading army and navy experts ridiculed the helicopter as useless and of no practical combat value. Today the chopper is one of our most valuable combat items. Besides having remarkable offensive value, it has even greater defensive value. It has rescued hundreds of downed pilots and has saved the lives of countless soldiers wounded in battle.

Kent goes on to cite other examples of how negativists have tended to block progress.

In the early 1950's the experts told Admiral Hyman G. Rickover that atomic energy could never power a submarine. Other experts said a ballistic missile could not be fired from one. But by the end of 1967 the U.S. Congress authorized 99 nuclear submarines of which more than a third are of the Polaris missile-launching type.

222

The development that has done more to change our way of living--the automobile--has been the target of numberless skeptics. The mere idea of a self-powered vehicle was ridiculed by the negativists, and every inventor who attempted a steam wagon or a gas buggy was laughed at.

When the auto finally made it, the doubters predicted failure for everything from the Kettering self-starter to the Oldsmobile front-wheel drive. Pneumatic tires, the doubters once said, would never hold air, and coil springs were "all right for mattresses, but for auto suspension--never!"

## Still around

Today, negativists are still blocking human progress. In our efforts to find ways to help the poor, the negativists are saying, "Why try to help them? They are lazy and will never change." In our efforts to help minority groups, the negativist throws cold water on whatever is proposed saying, "They are all a bunch of misfits, and they will always be that way." To our young citizens, who despise phoniness, and want to act honestly and courageously, the negativist says, "Why be honest and truthful, it will get you nowhere."

The seeds of the no-complex are in all of us. Perhaps the best way to keep them from taking root in us is to realize that the no-complex is a poison to personality growth and a block to progress. We will have to battle constantly to keep it from wrecking our lives and the lives of others.

125 Why is it particularly difficult for young people to keep from becoming negativistic today? Can negativism ever be sinful? What can a student do to keep from becoming negativistic?

## 81 "NEXT TIME I'LL RUN"

Author Vernon Pizer in "The Man with 8000 Miracles" tells the story of a remarkable man.

It was midwinter, . . . Seven-year-old Glenn and his brother Floyd were, as usual, first to arrive at school, and they set about building a fire in the potbellied stove. Neither knew that the Ladies' Literary Society had met in the school the previous evening, that somehow gasoline for the ladies' lanterns had got into the can that normally contained kerosene to prime the stove. The resulting explosion enveloped the boys in a ball of flame. Somehow they made it home. Floyd died. "Glenn," the doctor told the parents, "may never walk again."

After Floyd's funeral, the doctor returned to change Glenn's dressings; the burns were so severe he feared amputation might be necessary. He patted Glenn's shoulder and said, "When the weather turns warm we'll get you into a chair on the porch."

"I don't want to sit. I want to walk and run. And I will." There was no doubt in Glenn's voice. The doctor turned away.

After four painful months, scar tissue covered the wounds, but the legs remained useless, the tendons unresponsive, muscles tight, twisted, powerless. But Glenn was convinced those legs would again jump and skip and hop as a boy might command them. His mother, too wise to doubt the power of a child's belief, began a ritual of daily massage. For hours she kneaded the damaged muscles and flexed the legs. When fatigue forced her to halt, Glenn took over.

225 / personal realization

Six months after the accident, the doctor was transfixed by the sight of Glenn walking. It was a strange, limping gait, but Glenn was walking, unaided. The boy laughed. "I told you I'd walk," he said. "Next time I'll run."

Two years after the fire, the doctor did behold Glenn running--not fast, but running. Now he ran everywhere for the sheer joy of it. . . .

## What happened?

What eventually became of the seven-year-old? For the time being, let's not answer that question. Let's just say that the boy managed to live a normal boy's life in grade school and high school.

Eventually, he went to college, even though it was the heart of the depression and he was penniless.

But what about the original question? Did Glenn ever run again? Let's skip what Glenn did about running in grade school and high school, and tell what he did about it in college.

By budgeting his time carefully, Glenn was able to work his way through college and to run. No longer was he running to prove the doctors wrong; now he was running because he was good at it. In fact, he was great. Soon intercollegiate records began to crumble under his driving legs.

## National star

Then came the Olympics, which were held in Los Angeles that year. Glenn qualified for the 1500 meter run and placed fourth among the top runners in the world.

The following year, Glenn won the James E. Sullivan Award as "the amateur athlete who had done most to advance sportsmanship."

After finishing his studies at the University of Kansas, Glenn went to the State University of Iowa, where he got his master's degree. Next he started work for a doctorate degree in education.

Four years had now passed since the Los Angeles Olympics, and it was again time for this international competition to take place--this time in Berlin. Studies had not interfered with Glenn's running. Once again he qualified.

At Berlin that summer, despite a flare-up of his old leg injuries, Glenn broke the Olympic record for the 1500 meter event, though he came in second to John Lovelock of New Zealand. Glenn returned home to finish his doctorate. The very summer he received his doctorate, he broke the indoor mile record. "The boy who was not supposed to walk had become the fastest miler any-where, indoors or out."

126 What makes misfortune a stumbling block to one man and a stepping-stone to an-other?

Where now?

What eventually happened to Glenn Cunningham? What is he doing today? Sports fans frequently ask this question. Author Vernon Pizer provides the answer. It is even more fantastic than what Glenn did in the first half of his life.

. . . after wartime Navy service, Cunningham sat down with his wife, Ruth, whom he had met at Cornell, to consider their future. He knew that his need and challenge was to help unfortunate youngsters. Ruth shared her husband's vision. . . .

Returning to Kansas, the Cunninghams settled down on a beautiful 840-acre ranch they had bought a few years before, and Glenn went forth to aid youth. Ranging the country, he visited schools, churches, youth groups, civic clubs, to preach spiritual and moral values and perseverance in the face of reverses. His adult audiences were stirred by his mes-sage, his young audiences inspired.

Unbelievable

. . . [then], schools, churches, civic groups, social workers and juvenile courts have referred 8000 children to the Cunninghams. Some have stayed for weeks, some for years. The Cunninghams have never imposed a fee for the children's maintenance. They open their arms and hearts to them, counsel them, give them goals and the hope of reaching them, teach them to live with others in harmony and mutual respect, nourish their bodies and minds, and, most of all, love them.

But they never coddle; to each child they allot a fair share of duties and responsibilities. Foremost is diligent effort to become a proficient student in school. Other duties include helping in the fields or the ranch buildings, cleaning, raking, cooking, darning, painting. . . . [E]ach new arrival picks out his own horse. All the four-footed "therapists," Cunningham points out accurately, are raised on feed and love.

While devoting themselves to other people's children, the Cunninghams have not neglected to raise their own family--12 children, ten of them still at home. . . .

### Problem

But the financial burden of 8000 children is awesome. The Cunninghams' funds, once so substantial, dwindled. Four years ago, the Cunninghams reluctantly moved to a smaller, less satisfactory ranch 20 miles from Wichita. There they continued to accept troubled children, for Cunningham's cardinal principle is that a young life is not a commodity to be discussed in terms of expense. "Every child must have his chance," he says. "No child is basically bad--only environments and adult examples are bad. Change them and the goodness in the child shines through."

### Help

Last year, a group of Wichita's leading citizens got together to relieve the Cunninghams of their financial burden. They incorporated the ranch as a nonprofit foundation, freeing Cunningham for unworried devotion to the children. At the moment the foundation is negotiating for a new, 160-acre tract on a lake, because present facilities are desperately inadequate.

Judge James V. Riddell, Jr., Kansas juvenile authority and vice president of Glenn Cunningham Youth Ranch, Inc., says, "Glenn has an amazing capacity to inspire children. He stands before them as an example and as a goal, proof that the gravest handicap can be surmounted brilliantly. . . . He has long deserved more than merely our unbounded admiration, and now he is getting it--our help."

127 Would you say that the most remarkable part of Glenn's life is the first or the last half? Why? Why aren't there more people like him?

## 82 DOGGED BY DEFEAT

Defeat stalked him like a hunter;
it dogged his steps day and night.

| | | | |
|---|---|---|---|
| 1832 | lost job | 1846 | elected to Congress |
| 1832 | defeated for legislature | 1848 | lost nomination |
| 1833 | failed in business | 1849 | rejected for land officer |
| 1834 | elected to legislature | 1854 | defeated for Senate |
| 1835 | sweetheart died | 1856 | lost vice-presidential |
| 1836 | defeated for speaker | | nomination |
| 1836 | nervous breakdown | 1858 | defeated for Senate again |
| 1843 | lost nomination to Congress | 1860 | elected President |

Abe Lincoln knew defeat. For thirty years it shadowed him.
It walked the streets with him during the day. It went to bed with
him at night. Lincoln was well prepared to weather those shock
waves of setbacks that battered and bruised him during those
bloody Civil War years. Another man might have collapsed under
the ordeal. But not Abe.

Shortly after his election, Lincoln said, "God selects his own
instruments, and sometimes they are queer ones; for instance,
he chose me to steer the ship through a great crisis."

God knew what he was doing.

128 How can defeat contribute
to a man's personality growth
in a way that victory cannot?

What may be a vice today could
become a virtue tomorrow.

### 83 YOU DECIDE

A Hollywood executive, Dore Schary, made this shrewd observation. He pointed out that a person's strength can frequently
become his weakness. For example, a woman who prides herself
on being frank and candid can easily find herself becoming tact-
less and cruel. A man who prides himself on having firm convictions can easily become pigheaded and close-minded.

Schary went on to point out that loyalty can lead to fanaticism,
caution to timidity, and freedom to license.

"All these," Schary said, "are ways in which strength can become weakness. But the reverse is just as true." For example,
daydreaming can be transformed into serious thought and meditation, extravagance can become generosity. Impatience with the
stupidity of others can be converted into determination to help
them. Discouragement because of one's failures can become the
launching pad for self-improvement.

What may be a virtue today could become a vice tomorrow. So
too, today's vice could become tomorrow's virtue. It's just a case
of keeping things in balance. And the only way to keep things in
balance is to weigh them occasionally in honest reflection.

129 Explain how frankness can
lead to cruelty. What is the difference between freedom and
license?

The Bag proved a point in a
dramatic and persuasive way.

## 84 THE BAG

Recently a college student made headlines by attending class
(a ten-week course in persuasion) covered from head to foot with
a black bag. The incident was so unusual that the instructor went
along with the Bag. A few of the students, however, were hostile:
What was the Bag trying to prove? What did enclosing yourself in
a bag have to do with a course in persuasion?

During the first weeks of class, the Bag suffered all kinds of
harsh language and behavior. Eventually the college newspaper
spoke up and defended the right of the Bag to be in a bag.

Meanwhile, the Bag kept his/her cool. He/She returned insult
with kindness. As the ten-week course wore on, the Bag ceased
to be an oddity. Hostility died out. The Bag was accepted as part
of the group.

The final day of class was spent discussing what the Bag had
proved.

130  What did the Bag prove?
Why did hostility die out? In
what sense is everyone in a
bag?

Everyone is different. No two people are the same--not even identical twins. The key to understanding and accepting ourselves and other people is to appreciate how different each person really is. Unless we appreciate this fact, we can misjudge people and make their own battle for self-acceptance and group acceptance much harder to achieve. Instead of helping them, we can actually hinder them.

### Voiceprints

In <u>Space</u> <u>Odyssey</u> <u>2001</u>, a science-fiction film dealing with the future, people are identified and classified not by fingerprints but by voiceprints. This is not fiction; it is fact. The sound pattern of each person's voice can be recorded and classified. When this is done, it is found that no two patterns are alike. Each is unique.

Fingerprints and voiceprints are not the only unique things about people. Each person also has a natural perfume about him that is distinctive enough for bloodhounds to trail.

But fingerprints, voiceprints, and odor prints are merely super-ficial marks dramatizing the uniqueness of human persons.

Far more basic are those biological and biochemical distinctions that make different people respond differently to the same outside stimulus. An interesting study of this is found in Professor Roger

232

J. Williams' book, <u>You</u> <u>Are</u> <u>Extraordinary</u>. He points out, for example, that one coffee drinker might say, "Those people who say
that coffee keeps them awake are merely faking themselves out.
It is all in their minds. I drink coffee and fall off to sleep immediately."

The fact of the matter is that these people are not necessarily
faking themselves out. It is a proven medical fact that the amount
of caffeine needed to bring about the same effect in two different
people may vary as much as ten to one.

## No faultfinder

Impatient reaction to temperature is also different in different
people. One husband may say to his wife, "This room is plenty
warm. You just imagine that it's too cold for you." Or an irate
wife may say to her husband, "You're the only one who complains
that my coffee is too cold or too strong. You're never satisfied.
You're always trying to find fault with me."

Again, the medical fact of the matter is that for this person,
with his unique physical makeup, the room or the coffee may
definitely be too cold. Ignorance of this medical fact can cause
us to judge others rashly and unfairly. It can lead to misunder-
standings that could be avoided.

There are scores of other examples of how people differ in
very specific ways. These range all the way from individual
nervous systems with different reactions to the structure of the
brain, which can differ even more drastically from one person
to another than do facial features.

Professor Williams draws some conclusions in his book. He
points out that all of this scientific information about individuality
is good news and has far-reaching implications.

Respect for the individual has always been preached. Every
human being has the same origin, destiny, and dignity; and is,
therefore, worthy of respect.

But biology and biochemistry are pointing to other reasons for
respecting individuals. These reasons can all be grouped under
a basic one: It is because each individual is not the same, but
very different.

131 Would you say that ignorance
of the uniqueness of persons or
groups is responsible for much
intolerance in today's society?

## 86 DOING YOUR THING

The story of a man who won
instant fame but lost himself.

Some years ago Robert Benchley, a writer, decided to become
a comedian. He won instant popularity and fame. Few people
realized, however, that Benchley would have preferred to write
rather than tell jokes. It was only after his death that the true
facts became known. In the book, Robert Benchley: A Biography,
Benchley's son writes:

He [Dad] would have preferred to be fairly well known as
a writer rather than very well known as a movie and radio
comedian. The only trouble was that the movie and radio work
paid much more money, and wasn't anywhere near as hard as
writing had become . . . The sleeping pills that he took at night
kept him awake, and the Benzedrine that he took on the movie
lot made him drowsy, and he finally gave up taking the Benzedrine
because he could think of no particular reason for wanting to
stay awake anyway.

Robert Benchley died at the age of 56--a rather unhappy man.

132 What does this story of
Robert Benchley have to do
with doing your thing? To what
extent can money or fame substitute for doing your thing?

234

Christ and you

Christ frequently referred to the importance of discovering
and using your talents to the full. For example, Matthew 19:
16-22 tells about a talented young man who came to Jesus for advice on how to live his life. Jesus advises him. The young man
listens carefully, but decides not to follow Jesus' advice. Result:
the young man "went away sad." He was never heard from again.
    In Matthew 25:14-30, Jesus tells a parable about three men
who receive different amounts of money (talents) to work with.
Two of the men use the money wisely. The third does not. Result:
the fate of the first two men is a happy one; the fate of the third
is sad.

> 133 Bob says, "I realize I have
> a lot of talent, but if I worked
> like I should at developing it,
> I'd miss out on a lot of fun.
> Life would become one big
> bore." Comment.

Question

During a discussion of the Benchley incident, a student came
up with this excellent question:

Does doing your thing mean that you are made to do only one
thing, and your happiness is determined by whether or not
you find and do that thing? I don't think that this is the point of
the Benchley story. Certainly writing is a lot different from
acting in the movies. My question is this: "How narrow is
your thing?"

> 134 How would you be inclined
> to answer this boy's question?

## 87 DANCING IS HELL

Walter Terry in "Man Who Dances"
describes a TV show that dared to
tell it as it is.

Night after night we watch TV. We see shows, but we rarely
see the show behind the show. This is unfortunate for, at least,
two reasons.

First of all, we miss out on the important fact that good shows
don't just happen. They are carefully planned and often take months
--even a year to prepare. Knowing this fact greatly heightens our
personal appreciation of the show that we are viewing.

Second, we would learn an important fact about the performers
in the show. Like good shows, good performers just don't happen.
They are men and women who have paid a high price for their skill.

The following excerpts from "Man Who Dances," will give us a
better appreciation of the fact that hard work--even painfully hard
work--lies behind any great human achievement.

Trade secrets

Dancers--at least all of those I talked with--hated the
greatest documentary of the decade. It was the Bell Telephone
Hour's television special, <u>Man Who Dances</u>: <u>Edward Villella</u>,
featuring the star of the New York City Ballet. I know why they
hated it, and I sympathize. The show was . . . a revelation
of pain and anguish and even terror. To some dance beholders,
this was naughty, like giving away trade secrets. To other

dancers who saw it, the scenes of Villella doubled up with fatigue, falling on stage (in full view of an audience) with muscle spasms, pushing himself beyond human endurance, were met with "So, we've all been tired, we've all been breathless, we've all had cramps."

Different reaction

Nondancers reacted differently. They were held spellbound by the course of events--not faked . . .

Theatergoers have no reason to know what a dancer's life is like--it is very much like a soldier's, . . .

Dancing is hell. Villella, in the Bell Telephone show, let us know this. What is equally important was that he let us know that it is worth it. . . . [A] dancer is very probably the most durable person in the world, one who needs applause and will suffer to get it.

The Villella TV show let you know that the boy had a letter in baseball and in boxing, that he was married, that he loved a good time. But the important thing was that it permitted us to see both the bone-deep pain and the ecstatic rewards of being a dancer. . . .

For nearly a year, cameramen had been following Villella about and taking literally hours of movie records of him performing . . . Robert Drew and Mike Jackson, producers of the show for the Bell Telephone Hour, studied the miles of footage, and they found a drama . . . They found they had a show. They also found that they had a dance documentary--clinical, intimate, and frightening--which had never before been recorded.

135 How would this show hold relevance for the boy who talked about the sophomore slump?

Jack Miles in "Tough Ten for a
Tough Teen" tells about a teen-
ager who "went for broke."

## 88 RAIN AND FLOODLIGHTS

No one took seriously Bob Mathias's bid for the Olympic Decathlon Championship . . .

After all, the 17-year-old high-school boy from Tulare, Calif.,
was entering the most gruelling test of endurance, speed, strength,
and all-around ability in the world of track and field.

. . . Bob Mathias was always a natural athlete, with coordination
that was the envy of boys several years his elders; at six he was
playing ball with 10-year-olds, and at 12 he was high jumping five
and a half feet.

But even into his early teens he suffered from anemia and nose-
bleeds which swiftly sapped his stamina, and he needed iron and
liver pills to overcome the "punies."

And although Bob was "Mr. Everything" at Tulare High--class
president, track and football captain, an 18-point-per-game
scorer on the hardwood--he had never run the 400- and 1,500-
meter races in competition. Nor had he <u>ever</u> pole-vaulted, broad-
jumped, or even <u>seen</u> a javelin.

. . . No one took Bob Mathias seriously--except Bob Mathias.
He made up his mind to go for broke . . . to become the youngest
decathlon winner ever. "When the pressure's on, I like it best,"
he once asserted.

During the summer . . . Bob worked to perfect his grip on the
javelin; three weeks before the elimination meet he began pole-

238

vaulting and hurling the javelin, following directions spelled out
in a track manual.

136 Why do you think Bob liked
pressure? Do you find pressure
a help or a hindrance in your
life? Explain.

At the Olympics

. . . The first day was dark and damp as Bob ran the 100 meters
in :11.2, broad-jumped 21' 8 1/3", put the 16-lb. college-weight
shot 42' 9 1/4", high-jumped 6' 1 1/4", and sloshed the 400 meters
in :51.7.

None of these marks, except the high-jump standard which
tied him with five others, was good enough for first place. But
he piled up enough points to rank third among the 35 entrants by
nightfall.

The following day was again rainy, and cold for August. Lon-
don's storied fog hung heavy over the field as the teen-aged mar-
vel stepped over the 110-meter hurdles in :15.7. Between events
he donned a rain slicker and huddled under a blanket on the wet
ground.

He gave the discus a mighty heave, but someone had knocked
over the distance marker and meet officials had to plod the soggy
field for two hours before they found it. Only then were they able
to declare Bob's toss the longest of the day, 144' 4".

Night had blanketed the city and the floodlights had been turned
on by the time the pole vault was called. Refusing to enter the
competition until the bar had been raised to 10'--the better to
conserve his ebbing energy for the two remaining events--Bob
cleared 11' 5 3/4".

An official had to mark the takeoff line for the javelin throw
with a flashlight, so dark and gloomy was it in that area of the
arena; but Bob's 165' 1" fling was tops for that challenge.

All he needed to win the gold medal was a halfway decent time
in the 1,500 meters--the metric mile. Every bone in his body
rebelled in agony . . . he was fighting off an upset stomach and
foot cramps . . . it was nearly midnight . . . and the crowd
had dwindled to a few thousand as the plucky youth half-ran,
half-lurched around the murky track.

His 5:11 clocking, pitifully slow, was nonetheless good enough
for a winning tally of 7,139 points. Competing against the best

athletes in the world, all of them several years older than he, he was the only contestant to exceed 7,000.

Worth it

He dragged his weary frame over to greet his parents and two brothers in the stands.

"Mom," he gasped, "how did I get into this? I wouldn't do it again for a million dollars. I've never worked longer or harder."

His mother, in tears, anguished, "I don't want my boy ever to do it again. It's too hard."

During award ceremonies the next day, however, she confessed to different emotions: "When my boy stood out there with 80,000 people at attention, and they raised our flag and played The Star-Spangled Banner just for him, I thought my heart would burst!"

. . . "You can't predict what he can do," one of his coaches said. "All you can be sure of is that he will win."

137 What role does sports and competition play in personality development?

## 89 THE POINT

Excerpts from a Wilson Sporting Goods ad in Time magazine.

This is your first game, son.
I hope you win.
I hope you win for your sake
not mine.
Because winning's nice.
It's a good feeling.
Like the whole world
is yours.
But it passes, this feeling.
And what lasts is what
you've learned.

And what you learn about
is life.
That's what sports is all about.
Life. . . .
The happiness of life.
The miseries.
The joys.
The heartbreaks. . . .

There's no telling how
you'll do.

You might be a hero
or you might be
absolutely nothing.
There's just no telling.
Too much depends on chance.
On how the ball bounces.

I'm not talking about the
game, son.
I'm talking about life.
But it's life that the game
is all about.
Just as I said.

Because every game is
life.
And life is a game.
A serious one.
Dead serious. . . .

Winning is fun.
Sure.
But winning is not the point.

Wanting to win is the
point.
Not giving up is the
point.
Never being satisfied
with what you've done
is the point.
Never letting up
is the point.
Never letting anyone down
is the point.

Play to win.
Sure.
But lose like
a champion.
Because it's not winning
that counts.
What counts is
trying.

## 90 HERO OR COWARD?

A student describes a challenge he
recently faced after a sports event.

I had just come out of the Western gym after we had beaten
Western by one point in an overtime period. Everyone predicted
there would be fights, but I did not really expect anything to happen.

As I was walking over to my brother's car, about five guys
cut in front of me. One of them came up to me as if to cause a
confrontation, but I walked a few steps to my left to avoid him
and reached the car.

The one who had cut in front of me before, now stood in front
of me and said, "What's your rap?" Not knowing the neighborhood lingo, I thought that "rap" was synonymous with "bag" or
"thing." I replied, rather stupidly, "Do you mean how I got these
numerals," indicating the "72" on my left sleeve. I did this because I thought he wanted to know if I was a basketball player or
what.

Undaunted, he replied, "Who won the game?" To which I naturally answered, "We did." Putting his fingers on my chest, he
asked again, "Who?" I now understood that he knew exactly who
had won the game, but he wanted me to say that Western had won.
Also, by this time, besides the six or seven youths originally
accompanying this one boy, there were roughly ten more guys
standing in a semicircle around me. (My back was up against
a tree.) They all waited to see what I would do. I neither backed

244

down and said Western had won; nor did I speak up to the guy.

Then a strange thing happened. To this day, and this is the absolute truth, I cannot recall how long I stood up against that tree, facing that band of angry youths. It could have been two minutes or two hours. I felt like I was floating around somewhere. I recall thinking a short prayer, but the most important thing on my mind was whether this guy had a knife or whether he was going to hit me.

Finally a senior from Western yelled at the guys to get away from me, and they dispersed. As I look back on the incident several questions keep bugging me.

  1  Was I brave or was I a coward?

  2  Why did I freeze up?

  3  What should I do, if a situation like this arises again?

  4  Is there anything I can do to increase my courage and self-confidence, both of which have been somewhat shaken by this event?

138  How would you answer the boy's questions? Take each question in order. Has anything like this ever happened to you?

## 91  BLACK HANDS

Roy Harrell, Jr., in "Congo Incident" looks at crowd-courage
from a different angle.


In October . . . I was on a flight to Brazzaville that was forced
to land in Leopoldville because of engine trouble. We were told
our flight would be indefinitely delayed and cautioned to stay
away from the city itself where there was great unrest.
    Nevertheless, I left the airport on foot determined to find
some way to reach my destination. I was doing research work
. . . under the auspices of the U.S. Library of Congress. My
next appointments were in Brazzaville which was not too far away
across the Congo River.
    Walking down the Avenue Albert Premier I noticed ahead of
me a group of native soldiers talking angrily. As I approached,
one of the soldiers grabbed me by the shoulder. I shook him off.
Then another knocked me flat with a blow to the side of the head.
Rolling out of their way I bounced to my feet. I ducked down an
alley, eluded the soldiers and sought out the American Embassy.
    News of my encounter with the soldiers had already preceded
me. Worried officials of the Embassy staff told me the soldiers
were angry because they had not been paid for some time. They
said it would be impossible to get transportation across the river
and advised me to return to the airport.
    What to do now? I remembered that in my records were the
names and addresses of two contacts in Leopoldville. Somewhat
to my surprise I was able to hire a car and chauffeur without

difficulty. We started out to find these people to see if they could help.

Driving beyond the Stanley Monument my driver pointed out a large home surrounded by gardens and a high iron fence. . . .

As our car passed the entrance some native soldiers rushed out at us. Without ceremony they dragged both my driver and me from the car. One soldier snatched an American Express check from my breast pocket, another took the film from my camera. Before I could protest one soldier hit me on the shoulder with his gun butt. For the second time that morning I was flat on my back.

Then a strange thing happened: as I looked up into the angry faces of the Congolese soldiers I found I was repeating to myself the words of the 121st Psalm, "I will lift up mine eyes unto the hills, from whence cometh my help. My help cometh from the Lord . . ." Although a regular churchgoer . . . I was not given to quoting Scriptures in emergencies. To this day I do not know why that verse came to mind in that particular tense moment. But suddenly my anger left me. I made no further effort to resist and remained on the ground, watching. The soldiers stood over me talking excitedly but did not seem to know what to do next. Finally, a guard from inside the entrance gate rushed out, pulled me to my feet and told me to leave.

Sore, bleeding, my clothes torn, I continued my journey on foot. A little while later I was in the market place.

As I stood hesitant on a street corner an African woman spoke to me, . . . "They are savages--all of them," she cried.

Then she took me over to a public water hydrant, wet a cloth and began bathing the cuts on my face. Soon other Africans were gathered around us and I was asked to repeat my story.

Suddenly a thought occurred to me, and I turned to the black woman with the gentle hands. "You had better not let the Force Publique see you helping a white man."

". . . I don't care if you are white or not . . . it's my Christian duty to help," she said simply. I was deeply touched . . .

Later that evening the ferries resumed operating and I left Leopoldville, happy, I thought, to forget the entire experience.

But I find I can't forget that gentle Congolese woman, . . . practicing her Christian belief in the face of mob violence.

139 How does this essay differ from the previous one? How can a student combat crowd-pressure?

Several students talk about the
toughest test a teen-ager faces.

## 92 CROWD-PRESSURE

Chris: Girls have a lot of pressure put on them by groups.
To be in fashion, to go out with a certain boy. If a girl wants
to stay "in," she has to do them.

Anne: There's a lot of pressure with regard to clothes, for
example. Also you have to dress like your friends, walk and talk
like them. If you don't, you're not in. The best way to fight this
is not to belong to any group--to be yourself.

Linda: Other girls put a lot of pressure on you. For example,
some of your friends want to try pot and they'll keep asking you
to join them, giving you all kinds of inadequate reasons, like
"think of the experience." Everyone has to be an individual. Make
yourself a promise to do what you want. If you have conviction,
it won't be long before they will start respecting you for it.

Nancy: There is a great pressure to smoke. A girl is considered
immature, a child who is afraid to get caught or just plain scared to
try. One way to rebel against this is to tell yourself that you are
not what they say you are, for only you know what you're really like.

Jan: In matter of dress, I conform. As for morals, beliefs,
and things like that, I feel that I set my own norms. My ideas differ
from a lot of my friends. To combat pressure, you have to be set
and convinced of the worth of your own ideas.

Reni: No pressure is put on me. I'm my own person and all who
know me know this. They don't push me because I don't bounce easily.

248

Jack: Combatting group pressure is one of the hardest things
a teen-ager faces. Do you know what happens when you fight group
pressure? You usually become a lonely kid, and loneliness is a bad
state to be in. Once in a while I get that feeling--that I don't have
a friend in the world--and it's pure hell.

Pete: There is no special formula to fight the pressure. You
just have to have guts and stick it out. You have to have patience
and strength and be able to take being called chicken for a while.
It will not last long, although it might seem like ages. Pretty soon
the group will realize where you stand, and they won't bug you anymore. In fact, they will respect you for sticking to your guns.

Bill: I think each individual will have to combat group pressure
in a different way. What works for one person, may not work for
another. The important thing is that you must have strong convictions. A lot of teen-agers have not yet formed convictions on
many things--much less strong ones.

Joe: You also have to have the courage of your convictions.
You can have all the convictions in the world, but if you don't
have the courage, you're dead.

140  Who made the best point?
How might different people combat pressure in different ways?

## 93 BUCKING THE CROWD

A junior ponders the need for people to stand up and speak out.

Edmund Burke once said, "All that is required for the triumph
of evil is that good men remain silent and do nothing."

Everyone has had the opportunity to stand out from the crowd
and to help someone in need. But how many have taken advantage
of this opportunity? Not many! Why?

Lord, help us to find our own answer to this disturbing question. Teach us also:

to serve you as you deserve;
to give and not to count the cost;
to fight and not to heed the wounds;
to toil and not to seek for rest;
to labor and not ask for reward.

To help is to love. To love is to live.

141 List some of the reasons
that people give for not speaking out against evil. Discuss the
pros and cons of each reason.

## 94 TELESCOPE EYES

Teacher Ralph Prouty in "Student
Cheaters" talks to parents about
a big school problem: cheating.

Cheating in high school is increasing, and is jeopardizing
many students' chances of ever getting into college. A survey
by Columbia university indicates that in some 100-odd uni-
versities, about half the students cheated regularly. This 50%
represents an increase since the last survey several months
ago. Prof. Philip E. Jacob of the University of Pennsylvania
then reported cheating among 40%.

Bigger problem

More alarming than the percentage is the fact that cheaters
seldom had any sense of wrongdoing. Dishonesty had become
part of their lives. They felt they were entitled to everything
they could get away with. This attitude begins in grade school,
becomes widespread in junior high, and is a major problem
by senior high.

Studies of cheating made by several colleges, the University of Texas, Brigham Young, Purdue, San José State, reveal a tendency toward increase of cheating in succeeding
grades. By 5th grade, one third of a class may be regular
cheaters. In junior high the number may have risen to 40%;
by senior high to 50% or more.

In 20 years of teaching high-school English, I have seen an astounding number of cheaters and methods of cheating. It is not just a matter of a student cheating on his own test. When he leaves class, he may tell his friends, who will take the exam later, what questions to expect.

No one has yet suggested that cheaters are born. They are created, by motives and pressures. The problem is a matter of fundamental honesty.

## Learning to cheat

The child learns his concept of honesty from his parents, not from pious maxims but from your example. You may keep him out of school to visit Aunt Inez in Centerville, and the next day write his teacher a note that he had an upset stomach. Do you think your child isn't aware of your dishonesty? When you lie to the ticket seller at the movies to slip your child in for half price; when you boast about fixing a traffic ticket or padding an expense account; when your son or daughter hears you bragging about how you doctored your income-tax return, you are teaching him.

You are not merely committing dishonest acts, the child observes. You are also patting yourself on the back for doing it and getting away with it. The child can only imitate the person he respects most. If he has been brought up to believe getting away with something is the smart thing to do, a little thing like cheating in school is not going to bother him.

If you expect your child to be honest, show him how. By your actions let him know you expect truth and honesty in his dealings with everyone. You frown upon lying and cheating. Reformatories and prisons are full of men and women who mistakenly thought dishonesty the way to success. Your own life must be an example you will be proud to have your son or daughter follow.

This responsibility of yours extends from grave matters to many small details; it never stops. Jaywalk with your child? You're teaching him disregard for the law, so wait for the light. A clerk short-changes herself? Give back the money, and let your child see you refuse to take something that doesn't belong to you.

Honest students can be led into cheating habits by teachers. If students feel that the work is too hard, or that it is pointless, they may cheat. If they think the teacher is simply trying to keep them busy, they may take the attitude that cheating isn't really dishonest but just a way of getting even with an unfair teacher.

252

An important cause of cheating is pressure to make grades. The student finds himself caught in the middle between parents and school, both of whom are pressuring him.

If the student is given good grades, he gets a reward. The parents make a happy fuss, privileges are granted, and life is good. But let the student bring home a poor report card, and things change. For the next six weeks--no dates, no car, no television.

Some parents pay their children for each A they get on report cards. I've known cases where the father offered $5 for each A. Is it surprising that some children cheat?

Students now have a new attitude toward the honor roll. Formerly only squares and grinds were concerned with getting on it. Now it is a status symbol. If your name is not on it, you do not belong. You are not in with the crowd. That is another pressure for better grades.

These pressures extend beyond high school and college. Employers, the federal government included, assume that grades indicate ability. A college degree therefore brings higher status, greater responsibility, better pay. The ambitious student might figure, "If I have to do some cheating to get the degree, where's the harm?"

Such a philosophy of life carried to its logical end can be a disaster. Writer-editor Jerome Ellison comments, "The space age demands rockets that will work, and they will not be produced by designers who won their A's in math by cheating. The surgeon at the operating table needs knowledge, not just a grade."

Remedies?

Many schools have reasoned that if the grading system results in undue pressure on the student we should do away with grades. Today, in many schools there is no A, B, C, D, or E. The pupil merely passes or fails the course. There is still bound to be some pressure to pass, but it is nothing compared to the usual demand for higher grades.

William Graham Cole, chairman of the Department of Religion at Williams college, suggests that our American educators adopt the tutorial system, so effectively used in England for many years. The essence of this method is that one teacher works closely with a student to prepare him for an examination to be given by someone else.

Widely recommended by many educators is the honor system.

However, it tends to break down once a certain size and complexity of the student body are attained.

I hold that smaller classes are the solution to the cheating problem. If I give my students enough essay tests, I can tell whether they really know the answers. However, with a pupil load that varies from 165 to 200, a teacher can't do it. He is snowed under with paper work. A maximum class load of 100 students would allow us to do a proper job.

142  How widespread is cheating in this school? Is copying homework the same as cheating? How can cheating be cut down?

## 95 WHO GETS HURT?

Is cheating really so bad? Here is what some have said about it.

1 Cheating weakens your character. You get into the habit of taking the easy way out. You also pave the way for cheating in bigger things later.

2 It hurts other people. By your unfairness you deprive others of a class rank or a class standing that they have worked hard for and justly deserve.

3 It makes you suspicious. It is a fact that many people judge others by themselves. If they cheat, they tend to suspect that everyone else does. This leads to all kinds of rash judging of other people in other things.

4 It makes others lose trust in you. Cheating is a kind of combination of stealing and lying. You steal answers from someone else. You then deceive the teacher by making him think that the answers are yours.

143 Of the above effects, which do you think are most serious? Least serious? How would you go about breaking a serious cheating habit?

Eight boys tell what they most admire and look for in a girl.

## 96 BOYS DISCUSS GIRLS

Lou: I look for someone who is fun to be with. If she isn't fun to be with, I tend to lose interest.

Jack: What I look for in a girl is honesty--not in the sense of not lying. But in the sense that she doesn't pretend to be something that she isn't.

Den: Give me looks! Also, one who is not uptight, who makes me feel good and will do the things I want to do.

Murph: A girl can either bring out the best or the beast in a guy. I admire the girl who affects a guy in a good way.

Tim: Look for personality first. Looks come second for the simple reason that looks neither talk to me nor understand me. I expect a girl to understand me as she expects me to understand her. Nor should a girl put herself on a pedestal. The guy is the one who puts her there. If a girl has person- ality (she needn't be a great conversationalist) and has looks (she needn't be a beauty

queen), and if she doesn't put
herself on a pedestal, she'll
soon find someone who will.

Ted: I don't look for just one
thing, but a combination of things
--attractiveness and intelligence,
for example.

Mike: I like a girl who understands me and is willing to
accept me as I really am.

Pete: A girl should make
a guy feel wanted and needed.
That's what I look for most.

144 Which opinion do you most
or least agree with? Why?

257 / boy/girl relationships

## 97 INNER BEAUTY

Real beauty doesn't come out of a
tube. It is won, not purchased.

Judging from the beauty ads that choke our magazines and
TV channels, one might conclude that the secret to a girl's at-
tractiveness lies in expensive cosmetics. But Rouben Mamoulian,
director of such all-time hits as "Oklahoma" and "Carousel" says,
"No!" Real beauty--what he calls "second glance" beauty--does
not come out of a tube but from the soul. It is not purchased, it
is won. His proof is interesting.

He says: "Your every experience, every emotion, is automatically reflected in your face. The more frequently you experience certain emotions, the more permanently they etch
themselves on your looks."

Again he says, "Every time you do an unkind deed, whisper
malicious gossip, or belittle someone you create forms of mean-
ness and hardness in your face no facial cream in the world can
remove."

All of these discoveries by make-up artists only bear out what
Scripture has always said, "The beauty of the King's daughter is
from within."

Soul beauty

A beautiful girl has an inner glow. Real beauty comes
from within. That may sound trite but it's truth; otherwise

why are most women loveliest on their wedding day? . . . There is nothing exclusive about beauty. It is within the potentialities of almost any girl. . . . John Robert Powers.

When, at sixteen, I was vain because someone praised me, my father said: "They are only praising your youth. You can take no credit for beauty at sixteen. But if you are beautiful at sixty, it will be your own doing. Then you may be proud of it and be loved for it." Marie Stopes.

Physically attractive women are the most plentiful things pro-duced in America. . . . Yet . . . our national ideal of beauty is . . . as two-dimensional as the movie screen on which so much of it is projected. . . . Having painted thousands of women, I do not undervalue physical beauty; but without certain fundamental qualities of spirit, such beauty is a grass-cheap thing. Exactly, who is to blame for this state of affairs in America? . . . James Montgomery Flagg.

145  How would you answer
Flagg: "Who is to blame?"

Girls reveal what they most
and least admire in a boy.

Kathy: The thing I least admire in a boy is when he puts on a
front when he is around people. Even though he gets away with it
at first, sooner or later people will find out.

Teri: A little boy attitude is what I deplore! Never serious,
but always goofing around--treating the girl like one of the guys.

Casey: I least admire shyness to an excess when the boy doesn't
have to be shy. I also dislike the other extreme: boasting, thinking
he's the coolest thing around--and being too, too, too aggressive.

Karen: I hate most a boy who is all wrapped up in himself. The
superior "God's-gift-to-the-world" sort of a person.

Mag: I least like the ones who are rude--or those who take you
out and hardly say a word to you. Also the ones who goof-off with
their friends all night, or don't come to pick you up on time.

Barb: I can't stand the guy who thinks he can handle you like
a stuffed animal.

Chris: I hate a boy who lets me push him around. But if he
acts like he owns me, forget it.

What they admire

Shelly: The traits I most admire in a boy are concern for all
people and the courage to stand up for what he believes, but yet not
close-minded. He should be slightly domineering (especially over

domineering girls!). I also rate intelligence highly.

Greta: I personally like a boy who is truthful, even if what he has to say is going to hurt me. Everyone has his faults, so take it from there. But I also expect him to be courteous and thoughtful.

Elaine: When I meet a boy, I don't think I look for any special character traits in him. I look at him as a person and give him a chance to show me what he is like. . . . I can't stand phonies and can spot them a mile away.

Teri: A masculine man is as wonderful as a feminine woman. Masculinity covers just about all a girl wants and needs. A masculine man doesn't have to have the muscles of Hercules. Looks count, of course, but an average looking boy who is a tower of strength when a girl needs him is what I admire--a man who appreciates a girl's talents, moods, whims; a man who gives in just enough to show he's not made of lead, and yet not enough to be like a pile of wet noodles.

146 For girls: Which of the above comments do you most agree with? For boys: Did you find any of the comments surprising?

ACKNOWLEDGMENTS

American Red Cross Journal
    Travis, John M., "Contributors All"
    Wray, Irene, "Experiment in Brotherhood"
        Original versions published in the American Red Cross
        Journal; these adaptations by permission of the authors.

Ave Maria
    Konesko, Nancy, "Is the Teen-Swap for You?"
    Strickler, Patrick, "Another Afternoon"

Catholic Boy
    Miles, Jack, "Tough Ten for a Tough Teen"

Catholic Layman
    Prouty, Ralph E., "Student Cheaters"
        © 1966 by the Missionary Society of St. Paul the Apostle in
        the State of New York, and reprinted with permission. This
        article also appeared in the September 1966 Catholic Digest.

Chicago Sun-Times
    Boyden, Sarah, "An Awakening Interest in the ESP Mystery"
        Reprinted with permission from MIDWEST/Chicago Sun-
        Times.

Claretian Publications
    Clancy, Rian, C.P., "Mother Church Isn't Ann Landers"

Friar Magazine
    Kent, John L., "Watch Out for the Negativist"

Guideposts Associates, Inc.
    Harrell, Roy A., Jr., "Congo Incident"

Family Digest
    Hoag, Joy Marie, "The Mounting Problem of Teen-Age Shop-
    lifting"

Harper & Row, Publishers
Abridgment of pp. 21, 22, 29, 31-36, 38 in The Voyage to Lourdes by Alexis Carrel, translated by Virgilia Peterson. Copyright, 1950 by Anne Carrel. Reprinted by permission of Harper & Row, Publishers.

The Liguorian
Henry, William, "What You Oughta Do, Father . . ."
Lesco, Albert, "My Prison World Is Too Small!"
Mulligan, Elizabeth, "What It Means To Be Poor"

Media & Methods
Lambert, Robert, review of Manchild in the Promised Land by Claude Brown, in "Underground Paperbacks"

My Daily Visitor
Meditations from the June 1968 issue

Our Sunday Visitor, Inc.
"Father Conroy Talks to Youth," July 31, 1966
Cooney, Maurice, "The Challenge of the Priesthood"
Wiggins, Phyllis, "A New Member Speaks Out"

The Reader's Digest
Miller, Floyd, "The Angel of Hunter's Point"
Reprinted with permission from the October 1968 Reader's Digest. Copyright 1968 by The Reader's Digest Assn., Inc.
Pizer, Vernon, "The Man with 8000 Miracles"
Reprinted with permission of the author from the February 1966 Reader's Digest. Mr. Pizer's original article appeared in the Rotarian.

Saturday Review
Terry, Walter, "Man Who Dances"
Copyright 1968 Saturday Review, Inc.

The Sign
Hennessy, Augustine, "Faith Is More Than a Leap in the Dark"
McNally, Arthur, for an article from the January 1969 issue

Wilson Sporting Goods Company
Text from an ad that appeared in Time, May 2, 1969

## PHOTO CREDITS

Algimantas Kezys, S.J., cover, 6, 34, 79, 80, 91, 96, 116, 130, 156, 194, 208, 241; William Crowley, C.S.SP., frontis-piece, 13, 36, 42, 47, 214, 230, 249, 256, 261; St. Ignatius College Prep, 15, 20, 58, 126, 224, 243; Hales Franciscan High School, 30, 144, 162, 167; Art Dugan, S.J., 52, 88, 185, 202; Benedictine Priory, St. Louis, 64; Merton Classen, 70; Wide World Photos, 100, 108; Harold M. Lambert, 136; SK & F News Service, 176; United Press International, 236; Loyola University Press from Photographs /Algimantas Kezys, S.J., 34, 79, 241.

## TO THE STUDENTS OF
## ST. IGNATIUS COLLEGE PREP, CHICAGO

Father Link is grateful to the students for excerpts from term papers and homework. These student authors shall remain un-known to the public but etched in the mind and heart of the author.

# INDEX